WICKED WALES

THE APPALLING VICTORIANS

Catrin Stevens

Illustrated by Graham Howells

First published in Welsh in 2007 by
Gomer Press, Llandysul, Ceredigion, SA44 4JL
under the title *Oes Ofnadwy Victoria*

ISBN 978 1 84851 740 0

A CIP record for this title is available from the British Library.

This book is published with the financial support of the
Welsh Books Council.

Printed and bound in Wales at
Gomer Press, Llandysul, Ceredigion

CONTENTS

Introduction	5
Terrifying Terrorists in the Appalling Victorian Age	16
Kind Neighbours, Quarrelsome Neighbours	38
The Appalling Victorians' Scandalous Schools	41
The Crazy Customs of Wicked Wales	53
Would you believe it? Religion and the Appalling Victorians	73
Crafty Crooks and Painful Punishments	81
Old King Coal	87
The Glorious Gorsedd of the Bards	102
Barmy or Brave? That is the Question	110
Living History – in a Woeful Workhouse	113
Quarrelsome Quarrymen	116
A Gallery of Cool Characters	122
Fun and Games	133
This and That	139
Amen	144

INTRODUCTION

History can be really horrible. Just think of the long lists of boring dates your history teachers expect you to remember. Who wants to know the answers to: 'What happened on 10 November 1871?' or 'When did David Lloyd George cut his first tooth?' No one, except pathetically hopeless history teachers.★

And how on earth do they expect you to be able to answer silly questions like these about the Appalling Victorians?

★ The answers are blatantly obvious anyway:
On 10 November 1871, 'Welshman' H. M. Stanley met the famous missionary, Dr David Livingstone, somewhere in the middle of Africa and asked him the really stupid question, 'Dr Livingstone, I presume?' 'Stan the Man' wasn't much of a man, was he?
David Lloyd George was born in January 1863, so he probably cut his first tooth during that year. 'Ga ga!'

Yes, this is the horrible history of the Appalling
Victorians of Wicked Wales. But please don't read this
book in bed, or you'll have nasty nightmares about
murderers and rioters, scandals and strikes. Not
everything was hunky-dory when Her Majesty
Queen Victoria ruled the waves.

A CLEVER QUIZ ABOUT QUEEN VIC

1. When was Queen Victoria on the throne?

   (a) When she sat on the toilet.
   (b) After William IV and before Edward VII.
   (c) Between 1837 and 1901 (64 very, very, very, very long years).

2. Why did Victoria always wear black clothes and look so miserable?

   (a) Because she had to put up with horrible and hopeless history lessons too.
   (b) Because she was sad – Albert, her darling husband, died suddenly in 1861.
   (c) Because she liked making everyone else miserable.

3. What was Her Highness's favourite saying?
   (a) 'We are not amused.'
   (b) 'Whose sock is this?' (She had nine children and 42 grandchildren – that makes 102 socks a day!)
   (c) 'Newborn babies are very ugly.' (And she had so many ugly new babies herself!)

4. How many times did Her Haughty Highness visit Wales?

(a) Only once – she didn't know the way.
(b) She stayed in Wales for only seven nights during her entire reign of nearly 64 years (a lot of nights!). In 1889 she visited Llandderfel, near Bala, and had to endure a concert given by 10 harpists. She never returned to Wales. Do you blame her?
(c) She came on a Sunday-school trip to Rhyl every summer.

ANSWERS:
1b +c; 2b;
3a +c; 4b.

In 1897 Victoria celebrated her Jubilee – 60 glorious years (for her) on the throne. This is the scintillating song 'Myfyr Wyn' composed for the Wicked Welsh to sing on this awful occasion (I hope you won't be sick singing it!):

**Come, sing a song with me
And sound the Jubilee,
Now come, be quick;
Sing loudly, all day long,
A sweet and lively song,
To our beloved Queen –
Dear old Vic.**

And that's quite enough about the dreary life of Queen Vic. We can forget about her now and concentrate on the horrible history of Wicked Wales during her wretched reign.

Romantic historians claim that the Appalling Victorians lived happily in whitewashed cottages, with pretty pink roses trailing around their front doors. But that's only a tiny fraction of the truth, and in this book you will read about the rest – a truly incredible chronicle of filth and stench, terrible tales and crazy customs. So, we won't be mentioning sensational saints such as O. M. Edwards, T. E. Ellis, Charlotte Guest, Mrs Jones, Station Terrace etc. – only those amazingly brill people who make history so remarkably interesting. REMEMBER – YOUR great-great-great-grandmother and grandfather probably played a part in this stunning story. So, read on!

One prickly problem:

Some terrible things were said about the Appalling Victorians in Wicked Wales:

> Taffy was a Welshman, Taffy was a thief,
> Taffy came to my house and stole a leg of beef.

and

> Wales is a country up the backside of the world.

Charming! Unfortunately, many pathetic Welsh people thought these sayings might be true and spent a very long time trying to prove they were wrong.

Read this horrid history and YOU decide: are they true or not?

A TIMELINE FOR THE APPALLING VICTORIANS

1837

The beginning of this awful age – victorious Victoria (what a clever pun!) crowned Queen of England, Wales, Scotland, Ireland and any other country she could get her claws into. Hip Hip Hurray! or Help!? What do you think?

1839

The Newport Rising – the workers of Gwent, who called themselves Chartists, march on Newport to ask for the right to vote, and to make several other very reasonable demands. But 22 of them are shot dead – how reasonable was that?

1839; 1842–3

The Rebecca Riots – the fierce farmers of West Wales dress up as women to protest against having to pay road tolls . . . and against everything else. Farmers never change.

The beginning of the Railway Age with a railway built from Llanelli to Pontarddulais (or from Pontarddulais to Llanelli, of course). Before long the station with the longest name in the world was opened – LLANFAIRPWLLGWYNGYLLGOGERYCHWYRN-DROBWLL-LLANTYSILIOGOGOGOCH – Chuffing great!

1847

The Treason of the Blue Books – three useless English inspectors gather evidence from some ghastly Welsh people about the state of schools in Wales, the Welsh language and how Welsh women behaved (or misbehaved!). This report is published in large volumes with blue covers. The Welsh people feel they've been betrayed.

1848–9

A terrible epidemic of cholera – a very nasty disease which comes from drinking filthy water. The sick turn blue, vomit spectacularly, go to the toilet all the time and die within hours. In Merthyr (Martyr) Tydfil alone, 1,682 die – more miserable martyrs for that town.

1859

Thomas Gee begins to publish his famous newspaper, *Baner ac Amserau Cymru* (The Flag and Times of Wales). Soon, 50,000 copies are printed every week. This period was called 'The Age of Ink' (but not to drink!).

1859

A major religious revival sweeps through Wales. Bad men become good men; good men become very good men (the women are very good already!).

The people of Tregaron pour casks of beer into the river to show that they have now 'reached perfection'!

Hurray for the Revival. Hic!

Lead miners in Ysbyty Ystwyth meet underground to pray before starting work every morning (anything to get out of working!), and decide to stop swearing – the pit ponies are in a state of shock and unable to work!

1860 onwards

Coal, coal, coal – one coal mine after another opens in the south Wales valleys. Almost everyone is a collier or related to a collier. King Coal (sorry, Queen Vic) reigns supreme and the valleys are filled with black pyramids of coal waste.

1861

The first ever National Eisteddfod held in Aberdare. There'll be no escape from the drearily dressed druids from now on.

1865

A group of crazy Welsh people decide to leave poor little Wales to live in a much poorer country 7,000 miles away, far across the sea in Patagonia. *Hwyl*!

1868–1870s

Cardiff becomes the main city in Wales. In 1869 the first copy of the *Western Mail* appears. What a silly name for a newspaper printed in south-east Wales!

1870

An Education Act is passed to set up Board (not bored!) Schools throughout Wales for children under 13 years old. Bad news for every naughty child.

1872

A University College opens in a hotel on the promenade in Aberystwyth – a great place for hardworking students to chill out and enjoy a nice holiday by the seaside.

Where are you going on your summer holidays this year?

We're all going to the College by the sea!

1876

The first meeting of the Welsh Football Association. In their first game against England in 1879, six of the Welsh players were English.

1881

A law – the Act to Close Pubs on Sundays in Wales – is passed. But clubs are still open and people can buy beer there instead. Hic! Hic! Hurray!

1886

The Tithe War begins – more furious farmers who refuse to pay tithes to the church and to landlords. What a strange war – no one killed and only a few injured!

1898

The great Coal Miners' Strike – no more being nice to the Coal Owners. The crotchety colliers establish the South Wales Miners' Federation (the FED) to fight on their behalf. But the Coal Owners won't listen and the Fed becomes *fed* up.

1900–03

The Great Penrhyn Slate Quarry Strike. High and mighty Baron Penrhyn won't speak to the strikers, and the strikers won't speak to the 'scabs' who break the strike.

1901

Bye-bye, Victoria (by now, she had become a tedious old bore). Long Live the New King – Edward VII.

TERRIFYING TERRORISTS IN THE APPALLING VICTORIAN AGE

Rioting and rising up in revolt were the favourite hobbies of many Appalling Victorians in Wicked Wales. Read all about these terrorists IF you've got the guts.

Riot Number 1: The Scotch Cattle

Three fearsome facts about the crazy Cattle:

(a) The Scotch Cattle lived in Monmouthshire, not Scotland; they attacked goody-goody ironworkers and colliers who didn't want to go on strike and join their wretched riots.

(b) The leader of the Cattle wore a headdress bearing bull's horns; everyone else blackened their faces, turned their coats inside out and lowed and stamped their feet like mad cows.

I prefer Welsh Black cattle to the Scotch variety!

In 1832, 200 'Cattle' met to attack Richard Jerry's home near Nant-y-glo.

(c) The Cattle smashed windows and doors and broke furniture in the houses they visited. They killed a collier's wife in Blackwood (it was a black day for him, and her!).

But then, the Scotch Cattle disappeared like Scotch mist and Riot Number 1 stopped.

Riot Number 2: The Wretched Merthyr Rising

Fantastic facts about Merthyr Tydfil:

✳ Merthyr Tydfil was the largest town in Wales at the beginning of the Appalling Victorian Age (sorry, Swansea, Cardiff, Newport, Wrexham and . . .). But unfortunately this meant that lots and lots of people lived in frightful filth in tiny terraced houses. The snotty English snob, Thomas Carlyle, didn't have a good word for the town:

'It is like a vision of Hell . . . these poor creatures (toil) . . . in sweat and dirt, amid their furnaces, their pits, and rolling mills.'

Welcome to Merthyr Tydfil

And Dr Holland's description in 1853 was even worse:

Oops!

'In Merthyr I saw toilets filled to the brim – they weren't fit for use. People throw their sewage around everywhere and the pee flows down the steps to the court in front of their houses.'

✳ The filthiest part of this miserable town was called Chinatown. This was not full of cheerful Chinese people, but of sneaky thieves and pitiless pickpockets. The women of Chinatown were even more dangerous than the men. Would you like to bump into Siani Fawr Tomos, 'Snuffy Nell' Sullivan

But all I did was call you Siani Fach!

or Redheaded Betsy on a dark night? And even tiny babies were taught the art of stealing.

Lesson 1: How to steal another baby's bottle

❋ All these dodgy people had moved from the countryside to live in Merthyr and to work in the coal mines and the huge ironworks in Dowlais, Penydarren, Hirwaun and Cyfarthfa. The Iron King of Cyfarthfa was William Crawshay, the owner of the largest ironworks in the whole world! And where did he live? NOT in a filthy house in Chinatown, of course, but on the hillside in grandiose Cyfarthfa Castle, so that he could look down his nose upon his workers and the miserable town of Merthyr. The Castle cost £30,000 to build, but his workers' wages were only 75p a week. There were 72 rooms in this huge castle.

❋ Crawshay also owned many of the shops in Merthyr, and he paid his workers in tokens which they could only spend in his shops (clever Crawshay).

Then he could put up the price of goods in his truck shops, as they were called, and his wretched workmen would get into debt.

So, all in all, by 1831, the people of Merthyr had had a bellyful (well, not exactly, because they were starving with hunger) and the MERTHYR RISING BROKE OUT.

The Merthyr Tydfil Times

4 June, 1831   1d

A Revolting Riot

10,000 rioters on the streets

Scottish soldiers unable to keep law and order – 24 killed

THE REVOLTING RISING in Merthyr reached a climax yesterday. About 10,000 iron-workers and colliers came down to Merthyr High Street to protest, to break into shops and to attack people and steal their money. One of the leaders of the riot, Lewis Lewis (Lewsyn the Hunter to his best friends) said, 'We've got to riot to show the ironmasters that we have rights and that we can't afford to pay the huge debts we owe to the shops.' The rioters waved red banners and shouted 'Cheese with Bread!'

Scottish soldiers lay in wait for the rioters at the Castle Hotel. Suddenly, one of the soldiers fired into the crowd. According to Nancy Evans, who was in front of the hotel at the time, 'I heard these guns firing and saw everyone running away as fast as they could. When I looked around I saw about 100 people on the ground injured and some of them stone dead. It was a terrible sight.'

This morning the *Merthyr Tydfil Times* understands that about 24 people were killed and that 70 of the rabble and 16 soldiers have been injured. The soldiers and the police are busy now combing Merthyr for the unruly leaders. Someone will have to pay a heavy price for this revolting riot!

THE MERTHYR TYDFIL MARTYR?

And who was caught and punished for the rising? Richard Lewis or Dic Penderyn – not because he had the head (*pen*) of a bird (*aderyn*), but because he came from the village of Penderyn. It was DIC who was hanged for leading the riot.

But was he GUILTY or NOT GUILTY? You decide:

The evidence given by Donald Black
(one of the injured soldiers)

I don't know who hit me, but I saw Dic in the crowd in front of the Castle Hotel.

The evidence of Elizabeth Lewis
(she was in front of the Hotel too)

I think Dic is innocent. I saw him running away when the rioting began.

The evidence of James Abbot and William Williams – (two of Dic's enemies)

We saw him stab Donald Black. Oh yes we did! Things look black for Dic now!

The evidence of Lewsyn the Hunter

I led the riot. I was the one who broke into Joseph Coffin's house and I told the crowd to fight the soldiers.

(Lewsyn was found guilty and transported for life far away to Australia.)

And Dic Penderyn's own evidence
(he was a 23-year-old collier):

I didn't injure Donald Black. I wasn't even in Merthyr at the time. I'm not guilty – honestly! Please believe me.

Are you confused? Well, the Judge wasn't confused at all. In a cruel, gloomy voice he proclaimed:

Richard Lewis – Dic Penderyn, you are guilty. You will be hanged from the gallows!

And that's what happened:

August 13, 1831

Dic Penderyn was led out of Cardiff prison to be hanged. He was still protesting loudly that he was innocent.

Oh Lord, this is all wrong.

It looks all right to us!

When they were carrying Dic's body to be buried in Aberafan a cool white dove landed on his coffin! Was it trying to tell them something?

23

A frighteningly odd footnote

The evidence of Ieuan Parker in Pennsylvania, America, in about 1852-4

I have to confess before I die that I injured the soldier, Donald Black, in 1831. But I escaped to America. Sorry, Dic Penderyn.

Too late, mate! Poor old Dic Penderyn was the dead martyr of Merthyr Tydfil.

(By the way, I do realise that this revolting riot happened just before the Appalling Victorian Age – but it's too good a story to leave out!)

Riot Number 3: The daring Daughters of Rebecca

Every Welsh person thinks that he or she knows everything there is to know about the Daughters of Rebecca – the fierce farmers who dressed up as women and went out at night, not to enjoy themselves in a nightclub, but to smash gates and to do all kinds of other mischief in the countryside. (Well, they couldn't watch television and enjoy *Pobol y Cwm* or see the Queen Vic on *EastEnders* then, could they?)

You've probably heard a great deal about them, especially if you live in Carmarthenshire, Pembrokeshire or Ceredigion.

Isn't it strange that history teachers are so fond of these unruly rioters? If you tried to do what they did, you would probably be called a vandal or a hooligan.

In fact, there are several Major Mysteries which need to be solved about the daring Daughters of Rebecca. Read these silly explanations with a pinch of salt (and pepper):

Major Mystery 1:

Why did fierce farmers dress up as women?

- To hide their identity. They blackened their faces too. Well, would you be able to recognise your history teacher wearing a dress and with a blackened face? (Oops – don't faint!)
- Because they thought women were better at rioting than men. (Well, they're better at everything else!)
- To copy the crazy custom of the *ceffyl pren* (the 'wooden horse', but more about this on page 39). In fact they were drama queens. They liked to perform a pantomime when they came to a toll gate which blocked the road to market:

(It's as good as Shakespeare any day.)

Major Mystery 2:

Why did they call themselves the Daughters of Rebecca (or Beca) and not 'Gwenllïan's Girls' or 'Myfanwy's Maidens'?

✠ Twm Carnabwth, the first leader of the Daughters of Rebecca was a very large man, and the only clothes which fitted him were those belonging to Big Rebecca of Llangolman.

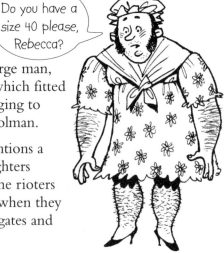

✠ Because the Bible mentions a Rebecca and her daughters looking after a gate. The rioters liked going to chapel when they weren't out smashing gates and rioting.

Major Mystery 3:

Why did the rioters attack the gates and toll houses of south-west Wales in particular? After all, there were similar gates in the other Welsh counties and no one attacked them.

✠ Because, from 1839 onwards, the greedy companies which owned the gates in south-west Wales erected new gates all the time and the farmers were fed up of having to pay the high tolls. They smashed about 250 gates in a year (five a week) – a world record at the time!

Come on – only one more gate to smash the world record!

Gate 249

✠ Because they were so poor it was easier to attack gates than it was to attack rents and tithes, the tax on the poor and every other tax they had to pay.

✠ Some of them loved a good old riot, especially those who had also been involved with the Scotch Cattle and the Merthyr Rising. What was one more riot between friends?

Major Mystery 4:

Who was Rebecca? That is the sixty-four-million dollar question!

Come on now, man, they can't all look like Rebecca, surely!

✠ Twm Carnabwth (Thomas Rees to his mam): HE was the first Rebecca, but he isn't mentioned again. Poor old Twm died walking down the garden to fetch a cabbage for his dinner! This pathetic poem, on his gravestone in Bethel chapel graveyard, Mynachlog-ddu, tells us what happened:

> *'Only God will know for certain*
> *What can happen in a day,*
> *As I cut a cabbage for dinner,*
> *Death stepped in and whisked me away.'*

And he didn't even like cabbage, poor thing.

✠ Michael Bowen of Trelech: on 19 June 1843, he led 2,000 of the Daughters on horseback into Carmarthen town. For the outing, he wore a curly yellow wig made of horsehair. In the town, the Daughters attacked the workhouse, where the most pitifully poor people lived, as if they were in a prison. But they didn't want their freedom! They refused to escape and join the Rebecca Rioters.

✠ Hugh Williams, a solicitor from Carmarthen. He didn't go out rioting, but perhaps he was the MASTERMIND planning the whole campaign. He was too clever to be caught (probably just like YOU when you misbehave in your history lessons).

So who was Rebecca? Who knows? This is the most maddening mystery of all.

Major Mystery 5:

Why did the riots come to an end so suddenly in the autumn of 1843?

✠ Things were turning nasty and people were being killed and injured:
  - the woman who kept the toll house in New Inn, Ceredigion, was shot and blinded.
  - the old lady in charge of Tŷ Coch gate near Neath was severely injured.
  - Sarah Williams, aged 75, was murdered in Hendy toll house, near Pontarddulais.

  It all ended in tears.

✠ At last, important government officials came down to listen carefully to the furious farmers' complaints and to try to sort them out.

✠ They caught some of the unruly rioters and punished them. One of these was Dai *Cantwr* (Dai the singer), who was transported to Australia. He loved singing ballads, and before he went he may have sung a silly song like this:

> *Farewell, my dearest country,*
> *I'm sorry I've been so bad,*
> *My heart it breaks with* hiraeth,
> *I'm feeling really sad;*
> *Bye-bye, dear friends and family,*
> Hwyl fawr, *ta-ta, so-long,*
> *Rebecca's daughter is sailing*
> *Far away from the 'Land of Song'.*

Boo hoo. I've left my teddy in Wales.

Poor Dai died in Tasmania in 1874. He set his bed on fire with his pipe and burned to death (no longer Dai *Cantwr* but Dai Death!).

And that's the end of the horrid history of the daring Daughters of Rebecca.

Riot Number 4: The Chartists and their *twp* tic-tacs

The Chartists were another gang of rebellious rioters during the Appalling Victorian Age – and all they ever asked was for the Government to accept their PEOPLE'S CHARTER.

Your history teacher probably adores the Chartists, and almost certainly loves to torment the class, expecting everyone to know all SIX points of the PEOPLE'S CHARTER. But why don't YOU torment your teacher in return, to see whether HE or SHE can remember all SIX points. He'll start to blush, then his face will go as white as a sheet, and he'll start mumbling incoherently like this:

Point 1: Every man to be allowed to vote (no mention of women of course); Point 2: A secret vote (instead of voting by raising your arm and then being punished); Point 3: Elections to be held every year (help!); Point 4: um . . . um . . . um . . .

Your teacher will be absolutely flummoxed, and will have completely forgotten the other three points.

Then you can look very important and reel off the last three (IF you can remember them, of course).★

But the Chartists' main problem was not WHAT they asked for, but HOW to achieve their aims. What trying tic-tacs could they try?

Tic-tac A

Collect names on a petition.
But unfortunately
most people couldn't
write at this time.
All they could do
was sign their names
with an X.

- In 1839 the Chartists collected 1,280,000 names on a petition;
- In 1840 they collected 3,317,750 names;
- In 1848 they collected 6,000,000 names, but among them were those of Queen Victoria and the Duke of Wellington – was someone cheating perhaps?

Parliament completely ignored these petitions (just the same as when you organise a school petition to demand more chips for dinner).

Very *twp* tic-tacs!

★ Pay MPs (point 4), who would not need to own property (point 5), and create voting areas with roughly equal numbers of voters (point 6).

Tic-tac B

Organise a revolt (the term for a tidy riot).

FORTUNATELY: Many of the Chartists were ironworkers and they knew how to make nasty and dangerous weapons. They could organise themselves secretly by speaking in Welsh.

What did he say? I wish I'd gone on that 'Welsh for policemen' course.

Wyt ti'n dod i wneud gwn, nos Fawrth? (Are you coming to make a gun on Tuesday night?)

By 3 November 1839, the men, women and children of the valleys of Gwent were ready to rise up in revolt and unite in attacking Newport (before going on to capture London perhaps?).

UNFORTUNATELY: It rained cats and dogs during the night of 3 November. In the fog and darkness, three armies of ironworkers and colliers marched down the three valleys into Newport (they didn't have mobile phones or iPhones then) and the whole march ended in a shambles. Two-thirds of the Chartist army decided to attack the town before the last third arrived.

The Mayor of Newport had organised 300 soldiers and 500 constables to defend the town.

The soldiers fired; the Chartists fired.

Result = MASSACRE

> SCORE:
> *Chartists: 22 dead; 50 injured*
> v
> *Soldiers: 2 injured*

(Almost the same as Wales's rugby score against England, a Welsh win, of course!)

The main Chartist leaders were caught, tried and sentenced:

John Frost, Zephaniah Williams and William Jones – you are GUILTY of treason (that is, being a traitor against Queen Vic herself). All of you will be taken by sledge to be hanged. Then we'll chop off your heads and divide your bodies into four quarters. The Queen will decide what to do with these bloody bits.

SO, WERE THESE TIC-TACS TOTALLY *TWP*?
Um . . . um . . . perhaps not, after all.

Instead of being hanged, Frost, Williams and Jones's lives were spared and they were transported to Australia for life. But, in 1856, John Frost returned to Britain and received a pardon. By then he had become a heroic hero, and if you visit Newport today you will see a square (not a triangle!) named after him.

And, in the end, we know that Parliament passed and accepted five of the six points of the People's Charter. What were they again?

Riot Number 5: The Wondrous Tithe War

This wasn't a pathetic little riot or a wretched revolt but a wondrous WAR. But who fought whom?

'I am the Reverend Ponsonby-Pugh B.A. (Bad Apple) B.D. (Boring Dunce) – vicar of the parish of Llanufudd, Denbighshire. You, John Jones, must pay your tithes to the church. That will be £6 14s please.'

'But I'm only a small tenant farmer. I can't afford to pay one tenth of what I earn to the church this year, sorry. And anyway I don't go to church – I go to chapel.'

'Nonsense! Come along now, man! If you don't pay up I'll have to take a cow worth £6 14s from your farm.'

'You'll have to fetch it yourself then.'

'I'll bring 100 policemen and soldiers to help me. I'll win this war.'

'Oh no, you won't! I shall sound the tithe horn and all the farmers in the area will race to the farm to help me. WE WILL OVERCOME!'

'But we'll have guns and clubs – Ta-ra-ra-ra-ra!'

'And we'll have bad eggs, stones, rotten potatoes and cow dung. Take that!'

SPLAT!

Yes, that was the wondrous Tithe War, which went on from 1886 until 1892. (Let's hope the farmers had enough fresh cow dung to last them six years!)
The tenant farmers WON. And after 1891 they didn't have to pay tithes to the church any more.

What a very strange war – or was it just a storm in a teacup?

KIND NEIGHBOURS,
QUARRELSOME NEIGHBOURS

In Wicked Wales the Appalling Victorians loved getting up one another's noses.

Ouch!

If a fierce farmer fell out with another fierce farmer, he liked to send along a stupid servant on a pitch-black night to:

- burn down his enemy's haystack
- break his horses' legs
- steal his sheep and drive them into the river to drown.

I told you to break its leg, not pull its leg!

But the most effective way of teaching a lesson to a disgraceful neighbour was to organise a pantomime called the WOODEN HORSE.

To ride the Wooden Horse you will need:

✓ a person you want to punish in front of everyone else in the village – someone who has been nasty to his wife perhaps, or a woman who has been gossiping about her neighbours . . . you choose;

✓ a large, angry mob carrying saucepans and spoons and making a terrible din to draw attention. The mob should paint their faces black and the men should dress up in women's clothes (but the women shouldn't dress as men!);

✓ a strong pole;

✓ a very, very ugly effigy (or model) of the person to be punished made out of straw and wood.

How to ride the Wooden Horse:

1. At midnight go quietly to the home of the person to be punished and drag him or her out of bed in his nightgown (no respectable Appalling Victorian wore pyjamas).

2. Make him sit on the pole – or the wooden horse – and march him round and round the village. If you want to, you can carry the straw effigy too, to frighten everyone out of their wits.

3. Make as much noise as possible to wake everyone up. You can sing this little ditty:

Wham! Bang! Bang! Wham! Bang! Bang!
We're here for Betty Morris's man!
We'll give him the hardest blows we can!
We'll mock him and poke him with such force:
We'll make him ride the Wooden Horse.

But I don't even like singing 'Ride a Cock Horse to Banbury Cross!'

4. When you've finished mocking him, take him home. He won't misbehave ever again.

Everyone was afraid of the wild Wooden Horse – especially the vile victim who was being punished!

THE APPALLING VICTORIANS' SCANDALOUS SCHOOLS

TODAY:

Tick ✓ the box if your splendid school has:

a brill building ☐   books ☐
electricity ☐   toilets ☐
heating ☐   school grounds ☐
desks/tables ☐   teachers who are OK ☐
        and have been to college

Marks: probably **8/8**.

THE APPALLING VICTORIANS:

At the beginning of the Victorian Age there weren't many schools in Wales. There was no electricity, no proper heating, and nothing much else in these schools and very few children attended them.

Marks: **0/8**.

The Rotten Report of 1847

In 1847 a really rotten Report about the state of Welsh schools was published. It was written by three wise men from England, who knew nothing about schools or about Wales. Here are some of the most unpleasant and unfair things they said (you should sit down comfortably to read these dreadful descriptions, in case you feel queasy):

First Wise Man: Lingen

This school is held in the teacher's home. I shall never forget the hot sickly stench which hit me when I opened the door to this low dark room, where 30 girls and 20 boys were huddled together.

Second Wise Man: Symons

The school was horrendous: the only furniture they had was one very wretched table; a few broken benches; the floor was full of holes and the room was very dark.

Third Wise Man: Vaughan-Johnson

The boys' school was held in the most atrocious hovel – rain poured in through the thatched roof. Of the 629 schools I have seen, 364 of them had no toilets whatsoever (ych-a-fi).

And to cap it all, the teachers were absolutely useless:

In Llanfair-is-gaer school, Gwynedd, the teacher was a shopkeeper. He had been injured and he thought that teaching would be much easier than serving in a shop. (Ask your teachers what they think of this!)

The tedious teacher in Cilcain, Flintshire, was an injured coal miner. He couldn't speak English – poor thing – but his Welsh was excellent.

And according to the THREE WISE MEN, teaching was:

The job people respected least of all and the one with the lowest wages. This job is for those who have failed to do anything else worthwhile!

(Don't show this to your teachers or they will probably sulk forever.)

So these were the main problems in the scandalous schools of Wales according to this rotten Report. It was published, between pretty blue covers, on 1 April 1847. But the wicked Welsh couldn't see the joke, especially when they had read it from cover to cover.

ATROCIOUS ALLEGATIONS

But there were even more atrocious allegations in the rotten 1847 Report. Perhaps the three wise men from the east (England is in the east) did state some home truths about some Welsh schools, but the other allegations they made about Wicked Wales were appalling.

ABOUT THE PEOPLE

Flint – the streets of this town are filthy: the houses have been very badly built; the people are grubby and dressed in rags. Drunkenness is the worst offence and this is because Welsh people like going to the *Noson Lawen* (Merry Evening).

ABOUT THE WOMEN

Merthyr – the women of Merthyr gather in one another's homes to drink tea every afternoon at four o'clock, to gossip and chit-chat, instead of making food for their husbands.

The women of Llanelli are untidy and wasteful – they're very foolish mothers.

I've heard that all the women of Merthyr do is drink tea in one another's homes and gossip all afternoon.

Jiw, jiw. You don't say!

Thank goodness we're not like them.

ABOUT THE WELSH LANGUAGE

The most atrocious allegations were made against the Welsh language.

The Reverend James Hughes of Llanhilleth told Symons:

The Welsh language is a great disadvantage to the people of Wales. Nothing of any value has been written in it. I think the language is a huge nuisance.

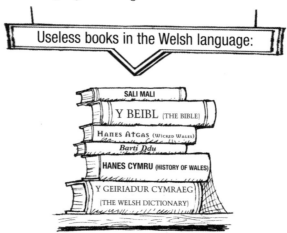

Useless books in the Welsh language:

SALI MALI

Y BEIBL (THE BIBLE)

HANES ATGAS (WICKED WALES)

Barti Ddu

HANES CYMRU (HISTORY OF WALES)

Y GEIRIADUR CYMRAEG (THE WELSH DICTIONARY)

Of course, some wicked Welsh people believed these awful allegations. And some of them tried hard to prove that the rotten 1847 report and its atrocious allegations were loony lies, fictitious fibs, and stinking insults against Wales and the Welsh people – and they're still at it today! Yes, this was the terrible:

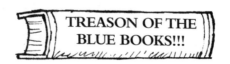

TREASON OF THE BLUE BOOKS!!!

LOUSY SCHOOL LAWS

Schools changed a great deal during the Appalling Victorian Age – perhaps <u>because</u> of the rotten 1847 report!

FOR WORSE:

1861: Schools were paid according to how pupils performed, not in a pantomime or a soap opera, but in THREE subjects – the three Rs – Reading, wRiting and aRithmetic. No mention of the Welsh language. Welsh would not be taught in the scandalous Victorian schools.

FOR BETTER:

1870: Board (not bored) schools opened so that every child under 13 *could* attend school.

1880: Every child under 13 *had to* attend school (so no more playing truant to go to the circus in town or to attend a nice little funeral).

1889: Secondary schools opened.

1891: Free primary education for every child.

PAINFUL PUNISHMENTS

The tedious teachers of the Appalling Victorian Age knew how to punish naughty children. They:

- made them wear a dunce's cap and stand in the corner

- locked them in the coal cellar or in a creepy cupboard

- sent the Kid Catcher or the Attendance Officer to look for them

- caned them (SMACK!) – on their legs, their arms, their backs, their hands and on their bottoms. The children thought that if they pulled two hairs out of their scalp (OUCH!), placed them on the palm of their hands and spat on them, they wouldn't feel any pain when they were caned. Unfortunately this trick didn't work quite so well on their bottoms.

Sorry, I was trying to spit on my bottom.

THE MOST PAINFUL PUNISHMENT OF ALL

Wearing the 'Welsh Not' – a piece of wood with the letters W.N. on it, which was placed around your neck if you spoke Welsh in school or in the schoolyard. But most of the children could only speak Welsh.

If you were a goody-goody you would spend your break wandering around the playground like a spiteful spy, trying to catch children speaking Welsh – and pass the 'Welsh Not' on to one of them. The pupil who was wearing the 'Welsh Not' at the end of the school day would be caned.

A PAINFUL PRANK

A clever-clog pupil in Tal-y-bont school, Ceredigion, tried to play a prank on his headmaster. This wretched man punished EVERY child who had been seen wearing the Welsh Not during the day – every child, except the one who was wearing it first thing in the morning. One day, this clever Dick said to his headmaster, 'Mr Jones, I haven't heard anyone speaking Welsh in school today so I haven't been able to pass the Welsh Not on to anyone. No one deserves to be caned today.' But, the headmaster wasn't stupid, was he? He thought the boy was too clever by half! 'I don't believe you,' he said. 'Come out here, boy and hold out your hand.'

Take this for not listening!	**SMACK**
Take this for not hearing!	**SMACK**
Take this for not using the Welsh Not!	**SMACK**
Take this because I think you're lying!	**SMACK**
Take this for lying!	**SMACK**
Take this to make sure you don't do it again!	**SMACK**

Now, get up on that bench, turn your back to the class. Take your trousers down. I'm going to cane you on your bottom next.

Take this for not listening! **SMACK**

SMACK, SMACK, SMACK, SMACK, SMACK!!!

. . . on and on . . . and on – 12 smacks altogether!

So please don't moan about your tedious teachers or your horrendous head teacher. Just be grateful that you didn't have to attend the scandalous schools of the Appalling Victorian Age.

ROBIN THE SOLDIER'S BRUTAL SCHOOL

In his novel, *Rhys Lewis*, the famous writer Daniel Owen describes the brutal school run by Robin the Soldier. Poor Robin had lost a leg in battle but he did have a wooden peg leg.

The story so far . . .

Rhys and his friend Wil Bryan played a nasty prank on Robin the Soldier in church on Sunday morning. They tied a piece of string to his peg leg and every time he tried to get up they pulled the string so that he came crashing down in his seat (BANG!).

But the following Monday morning in school . . .

Before long the silence was broken by the sound of the Old Soldier's leg pegging his way to school . . . The old warrior went straight to his desk, said his prayers (Our Father . . .) (Then) I saw him take out . . . a sturdy new cane. He looked at Wil Bryan like a bloodhound . . . he lifted his cane, but before he could do anything, Wil grasped his . . . wooden leg, hit him in the stomach and threw him on the floor. Wil walked out of the door. But I refused to follow him . . .

It was too late – the next minute the cane was cutting me in all directions – across my head, my shoulders, my back, my hands, my legs . . . Night fell – I became unconscious.

When I came to my senses I could see the Old Soldier on the floor, his face was purple and my brother Bob, in his work clothes and as black as a coal miner, was choking him. The other schoolboys thought Bob was the Devil himself when he entered the room . . . When Bob realised I was OK he released the Old Soldier, and we went home quietly.

If you tell your Welsh teacher that you have read Daniel Owen's obnoxious novel, you'll be teacher's pet and you'll have full marks in every Welsh test forever and ever – Amen!

THE CRAZY CUSTOMS OF WICKED WALES

In order to understand the Appalling Victorians we must know all about their crazy customs and their loopy lives. Read on, but only if you can stomach it, of course.

HAPPY HOMES

The Victorians loved to sing sentimental songs about their happy homes. This little ditty by Mynyddog (the Mountain Man) was the favourite:

> *'Oh, how I love my dear home!*
> *There's a magical sound to the word.*
> *Search east or west, my home is the best,*
> *There's no better place than my home.'*

LIVING LIKE A PIG

Unfortunately, however, not everyone lived in such cosy and happy homes. This is what one nosey visitor saw in Tregaron in 1847:

As I walked down the lane which is one of the main streets of the town, I saw a huge sow go up to the door of a house (the bottom half of the door was closed) and put its front trotters on top of the bottom half and shake it. A woman carrying a child in her arms rushed across the street from the other side, and opened the door for the sow. The animal squealed as it walked in, as if it was angry at the delay. The woman followed, closing the door behind her.

KILLING THE PIG

Everyone hated the day the pig had to be killed
(especially the pig). Somehow, it sensed that it was
about to be slaughtered and it would squeal and squeak
frantically (pigs can be very rude, can't they?). The
butcher would throw the pig onto a bench, stick its
neck with a huge knife (well, it did stick its neck out)
and blood would squirt into a bucket (by now the
squealing would have stopped, thank goodness). The
women would scrape out the pig's guts and rub salt
into the meat – to preserve it for winter. But by the
end of March it would taste like rubber.

It's bleeding like a stuck pig!

The Appalling Victorians loved their pigs because (almost) every piece of a pig could be used for something or other. Let's go the whole hog and choose which part could be used for what:

1. head   (a)   a ball

2. bristles   (b)   a present for a friend

3. skin   (c)   brawn

4. trotters   (d)   a brush

5. bladder   (e)   black pudding

6. blood   (f)   nothing

7. tail   (g)   *cawl* or soup

8. guts   (h)   shoes

Easy? Here are the dodgy answers, in case:

1 and c Brawn

To make brawn you must clean the pig's head, pluck out its eyes and cut off the ears. Then chop the head into bits with a huge axe and soak the bits in salted water for four days. Boil the head with the pig's tongue and kidneys for three hours. Chop the meat into tiny pieces and eat it cold. Mm . . . mm. Very tasty.

Let's make a pig's ear of this cawl!

2 and d; 3 and h; 4 and g;

5 and a Blow the bladder up into a ball and use it to play football (or if you can't get a round shape, play rugby with it);

6 and e This is how they would make a bloody black pudding on MasterChef:

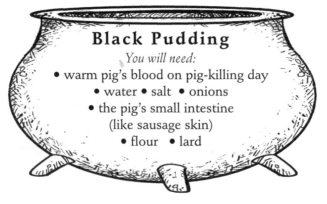

Black Pudding
You will need:
- warm pig's blood on pig-killing day
- water • salt • onions
- the pig's small intestine
(like sausage skin)
- flour • lard

Method

Pour the warm blood into a large bowl and stir well to prevent it becoming lumpy. Mix the water and salt into the blood and leave to cool overnight. Wash the small intestine. Mix the lard, onions, flour and cold blood together. Put the mixture into the small intestine and tie both ends. Boil the bloody black pudding in a large saucepan. Eat with bacon! (Snap! – what a piggish joke!)

7 and f Unless you like playing the game 'Sticking the tail on the pig' with your friends.

8 and b The guts are very *ych-a-fi*, so give them to your friends as presents. They won't be friends for long though!

PIGGLY-WIGGLY TONGUE-TWISTERS

You could practise saying this tongue-twister very quickly when you are making brawn:

'Soch, soch, soch – y moch bach gorau yn y byd'
('Snort, snort, snort – the best piglets in the world')

But take care – the 'chs' will make you spit all over the place. Easy-peasy? Try this one:

'Hwch goch a chwech o berchyll cochion bach, bach!'
('A red sow and six tiny, tiny red piglets')

A SWINE OF A SONG

And the Welsh were so fond of their (dead) pigs that they loved singing about them too:

> *'All you folks from town and vale*
> *Come and listen to our tale,*
> *It's a sad and sorry story*
> *For the end is very gory.*
>
> *Did you ever see,*
> *Did you ever see,*
> *Did you ever see,*
> *Such a woeful pig before?'*

And on and on and . . . for a further 11 verses!

A TINY TŶ BACH

Just imagine going out in the pitch-dark night, with a cart full of timber, mud, dung, turf and lots of beer – to build a 'one-night' house. It isn't surprising that the tiny *tŷ bach* (not the toilet) looked so awful when dawn broke. But if you could light a fire on the hearth and make sure that smoke was coming out of the chimney before dawn, you could claim that the house was yours (or that's what everyone thought, anyway).

Then you would look for the strongest person in the village – Superman or Superwoman would do – and ask him or her to throw an axe as far away as possible from the house. Where the axe landed marked the boundary of your land.

Unfortunately the owner of the land often came and threw the family out of its new home and demolished the one-night house. What fun and games!

LITTLE BOXES, LITTLE BOXES

So many of the Appalling Victorians moved to look for work in south Wales during this period, that they found themselves living in tiny terraced houses crammed one on top of the other in narrow streets. And then, their brothers and sisters would arrive to lodge with the family: Auntie Jane and her children would come from Caernarfon, a cousin from Carmarthen, an uncle from Swansea and friends from Ireland and Somerset – all wanting a bed for the night . . . until the house was chock-a-block. It would be so overcrowded . . . bursting with people.

In 1850, 54 people lived, ate and slept in ONE room in
17 Stanley Street, Cardiff. The pong was unbearable.

FUNKY FESTIVE FUN

Sending Christmas cards, enjoying a party around the
Christmas tree – this is how Queen Victoria and her
darling husband, Albert, celebrated Christmas in style.
But the people of Wales did things differently. Look at
this calendar of crazy Welsh Christmas customs.

Christmas Eve (24 December)

They didn't go to bed like good little children to wait
for Father Christmas to get stuck in the chimney.
Oh no!

They stayed up all night making very, very sticky toffee. You can try this recipe for Victorian toffee. But beware – boiling toffee can burn!

TOFFEE

3 pounds (1,200 grams)
of soft brown sugar
Half a pound (200 grams) of butter
Juice of one lemon
5 fluid ounces of boiling water

Method

Melt the sugar in the water. Add the lemon and butter and boil the mixture for a quarter of an hour, without stirring. Test the toffee by putting a teaspoon of it in a cup of cold water – if it hardens quickly, it's ready. Pour the mixture into a large, greased dish. Grease your hands well with butter and pull the toffee into long golden strands. Cut the strands into small pieces.

Eat it all and enjoy (but don't be sick!).

Christmas morning – the peculiar Plygain service (25 December)

They got up at five o'clock in the morning (it would be easier to stay awake all night) and walked to church to listen to one raucous group of clueless carol singers after another singing carols in the strange *Plygain* service. Many of the singers would have had a drop or two too much to drink beforehand – so watch out! – AND they carried lit candles. Playing with fire!

Christmas afternoon – a sensational sport for squirrels

In the afternoon, they didn't have pretty presents to open. Oh no! They went out to hunt the squirrel – the sensational Christmas sport. On one occasion, boys and dogs hunted a squirrel from tree to tree in the Llanwynno area. They threw sticks and stones to break its bones and the poor creature became exhausted. Suddenly, it fell from on high – straight into the open jaws of one of the hunting hounds under the tree. And that was the end of the squirrel (and the dog). What a spectacular sport!

Boxing Day (26 December)

A brilliant chance for men and boys to gather twigs of prickly holly to thrash the bare arms and legs of young women and girls – until they made them bleed. What was the point?

New Year's Day (1 January)

Boys would get up at the break of day – around three in the morning – and wander from house to house carrying a cup of fresh water from the well. They would splash water over the faces and hands of anyone who was still in bed (well, where else would you be at three in the morning?). Then they would shout 'Happy

New Year'. If the smashing splashers weren't paid for their efforts there and then, they would shout out spitefully, 'Have a dismal New Year, and a house full of smoke!' (What a charming way to start a new year!)

I haven't had a shower in bed before!

During the Holidays – the Merry Mari Lwyd

This crazy custom is still quite popular with frumpy folk dancers today. This is how the Appalling Victorians performed the Merry Mari Lwyd in Glamorgan many years ago:

You will need:

- A horse's skull – wait until the horse is dead – which has been buried in lime for a year so that the lime has eaten away its eyes and all its flesh (what **skull**-duggery!)
- A piece of wire to tie the jawbone so that it opens and shuts with a big bang
- A long pole stuck to the skull
- A long white sheet to hide under
- Black material to make ears; black glass for the eyes; ribbons to decorate the merry Mari and bells to make a noise.

And people:

- A **skul**ker, who likes to hide under sheets, to hold the skull
- A leader, wearing a bowler hat and tail coat, for the Mari Lwyd procession
- Punch and Judy, with blackened faces and dressed in rags
- A party of wild men who like making a racket.

What to do:

Go around the houses and pubs in your area to ask for (free) food and drink. Make as much noise as possible, shouting and yelling to frighten everyone. This is a rhyme about one such Merry Mari Lwyd:

> Pendarren's finest Mari Lwyd,
> The merriest ever seen,
> Bucked and kicked and danced its way
> Led by Sol Nant-y-ffin.

But all the doors will probably be locked against you. You will have to sing (in tune) for hours on end to be allowed in. The women and children will be frightened stiff of the Mari Lwyd, because she kicks and bites, she snaps her jaws and tries to kiss the girls. You don't have to be polite when you sing either:

THE MARI LWYD

Tonight, tonight,
You silly old bloke,
Your breath is so foul
It would stink through oak.

THE REPLY FROM INSIDE THE HOUSE

Tonight, tonight,
You look like a dog
You've the ears of a hare
And you reek like a hog.

(Can you write even more disgusting songs for your Merry Mari Lwyd?)

If two groups of Mari Lwyd singers met on the road, they would kick, punch and thump each other – neighing loudly – and they'd fight until bones were broken and blood flowed.

A Happy New Year, full of funky Festive Fun, to you too!

SIN EATING

If you died in Wales during the Appalling Victorian Age, you needn't worry (it was rather too late to worry by then, of course!). You wouldn't go to hell, even if you had lived a very, very bad life (not even if you had stolen your little brother's iPad or got on your mother's nerves). Your family would take care of everything.

1. Put the body to lie in the parlour.

2. Invite the village children to come and have a good look at it.

3. Bake a *teisen lap* (a very large Welsh cake).

4. Put the cake to cool on the dead body. (How cool!)

5. All the evil spirits and sickly sins will escape from the dead body into the cake.

6. On the morning of the funeral, give the cake to a poor old man to eat over the coffin.

7. Now all the sickly sins will enter into this poor old person!

8. And the dead person will go straight to heaven – a sinless saint.

Heaven's full of Welsh people. I wonder why?

It's not surprising that Welsh was called 'the language of heaven' in the Appalling Victorian Age, is it?

It would be a good idea to resurrect this custom. Why don't you go down to the shop now to buy flour, currants and eggs? Ready, steady . . .

WEDDING FUN AND FROLICS

Appalling Victorian brides loved teasing their boyfriends. On the morning of the wedding they pretended they didn't want to get married after all.

And so the bridegroom had to send the **shigouts** – a group of unruly rascals – to capture the bride from her home. When they arrived at the bride's house, the door would be locked and there wouldn't be any sign of her.

The bride would run to hide – under the bed, inside the grandfather clock, dressed up as an old hag, or up a tree in the garden ... what did her hair and her wedding dress look like after such an escapade?

At the very last moment the bride's father would hoist her up to ride behind him on his horse and gallop away like a bat out of hell before the Shigouts could get them – over hedges and through fields and rivers. Eventually, when they were all exhausted, the Shigouts would catch them and take the giddy girl to her bridegroom to be married – at last!

And everyone lived happily ever after – we hope.

TRIPPING OVER A BROOM

Some Welsh couples got married by jumping over a broom or besom. You didn't have to be an Olympic high jumper to get married in this way, because the broom would only be about 45 cm above the ground. But if either the bride or the bridegroom touched the broom, or tripped and fell head over heels (not in love!), the marriage would be considered null and void – tough luck!

What's going on here? Is it the Olympic 400 metres hurdles?

No, just a besom wedding!

AN AMAZING MENU

The Appalling Victorians ate incredibly monotonous and bo-ring food. This is illustrated really well in a story about Beti Jones of Ceunant, Llangwm, and her brood of churlish children. Are you sitting comfortably? This is her tiresome tale:

Beti was very, very poor and she had 25 fussy children who expected her to cook different dishes for them for dinner every day.

One day Beti asked them:

What would you like for dinner today, kids?

And these were the absurd answers:

Flour and wheat shot.

Oatcake in buttermilk, please, Mam.

I want porridge the same as Robin, no whey like Siân, no flummery like Twm, no . . .

Beti studied her favourite recipe book:

Oatcake in buttermilk

Contents
● *oatcake with no lard* ● *cold buttermilk*

*Crush the oatcake into pieces. Add the buttermilk.
Eat with a spoon.*

Cawl

Contents
● *Ham* ● *vegetables* ● *flour and water*

*Boil the ham in the water. Add the vegetables and then
the flour to thicken. Eat with a spoon.*

Turkey pie

Contents
● *bread* ● *boiling water* ● *a lump of butter* ● *pepper and salt*

*Pour boiling water onto the bread in a bowl. Lift the bread out and
squeeze the water out of it. Mix pepper, salt and butter into the bread
and eat with a spoon. But where was the turkey? (gobble, gobble)*

Beti closed her book. She fetched the ingredients for all 25 dishes. Then, she mixed them all together in one huge bowl.

She gave a bowl of this messy mixture to each child – *ych-a-fi*!

And that taught the cheeky children a nasty lesson.

(Beti would obviously have been better off writing a book about children's names, rather than studying useless recipes!)

Dear me, I've used up every possible Welsh name! What on earth shall I call this little one?

WOULD YOU BELIEVE IT? RELIGION AND THE APPALLING VICTORIANS

Squabbling and bickering

Although religious people are supposed to love one another, the Appalling Victorians in Wicked Wales had more arguments and rows about religion than about almost anything else. They were all Christians (one big, happy family) but there were different types of Christians (they called these *denominations*) and they fought and bickered all the time (just like you, your sister and your little brother in your big, happy family).

> Our church has the highest tower, so we must be nearer heaven than everyone else.

A member of the Church of England (in Wales!):
I don't like the Methodists because they're too noisy and enthusiastic.

Independent: I go to the Independents' chapel.
I don't like the Baptists because they don't allow

> Help!

babies to be baptised. They wait until children are 14 years old and then they throw them into a river or a bath of water (to be baptised – not to drown!).

Baptist: I go to the Baptist chapel. I don't like the Church of England because the members think they're so important and they're such snobs.

Methodist: I go to the Methodist chapel. I don't like the Independents because they are so bo-ring and, well, independent!

Unitarian: I'm a Unitarian. I don't like any of the others because they say that there are three gods in one – the Father, the Son and the Holy Ghost. But we say there is only One God – we're UNI-(one)-TARIANS. We live in the Black Spot (in south Ceredigion).

And they liked to shout vile verses at one another:

Heaven is full of Baptists,
The Water Baptists say,
For they're the only ones who know
The right and proper way.

Stupid Churchmen,
Heads so soft,
They built their church
Without a loft.

Independents,
Even worse,
Can't recite a single verse.

Nasty cruel Methodists,
With little sense of grace,
Sell seats to rich and wealthy folk,
So the poor will know their place.

I hope we can buy seats in heaven too.

But whenever the chips were down, the Nonconformists (the Independents, Baptists and Methodists) ganged up together AGAINST the Church of England.

But they had all forgotten about one other denomination. They were more afraid of this one than any other –

The Catholics:

You burned our saints and smashed our shrines
You sent us to the rack.
But look out, Wales! We're growing fast:
The Catholics are back!

And they were. Their numbers grew and grew – from 6,500 Catholics in 1851 to 65,000 in 1901.

A CYMANFA OF CHAPELS
SUPER STATISTICS

In spite of the bickering and arguing, new chapels
appeared like mushrooms overnight in the Welsh
countryside. A new chapel was built every eight days.

Where did that one come from? It wasn't there yesterday.

In 1846 there were 2,271 chapels in Wicked Wales.

By 1905 there were 4,280 chapels in Wales. Not so
Wicked now perhaps?

In 1900, 4,000 pathetic preachers preached 11,000
bo-ring sermons every Sunday. Sometimes one of these
preachers would break out into a song-and-dance
routine – *hwyl* – and the confused congregation would
shout: 'Thanks a bunch!' and 'Amen!' (though he never
took the hint!).

2,000,000 mind-numbing religious meetings were held
every year. And the Welsh people enjoyed every minute
of them. (Hallelujah!)

I wonder why the chapel schoolroom was called a *Vest*ry?

THE SENSATIONAL SUNDAY SCHOOL

This was the IN place to be. The whole family would be frozen stiff in a bitterly cold chapel or vestry learning to read and discuss – not fashion or football – but the BIBLE. In 1884, 10,000 Sunday-school members in Llŷn and Eifionnydd learned 2,181,410 verses from the Bible in a year. (That's over 218 verses each. Who was daft enough to count them?)

By 1901, a quarter of the population attended Sunday School. (The other three-quarters were fast asleep, and snoring soundly after a huge Sunday dinner.)

The teachers taught the poor children some very dodgy things. The frightful favourite was a set of questions and answers called *Rhodd Mam* (or Mam's Pet):

Question: How many types of children are there?
Answer: Two types.

Question: What are they?
Answer: Good children and naughty children.

Question: Which type of child doesn't listen to its parents?
Answer: A naughty child.

Question: Which type of child lies and swears?
Answer: A naughty child.

Question: Which type of child plays on a Sunday?
Answer: A naughty child.

Question: Where do naughty children go when they die?
Answer: To hell.

Question: What kind of place is hell?
Answer: A fiery, burning lake.

And after swallowing these frightful facts you had to remember:

REMARKABLE RULES ABOUT HOW TO BEHAVE ON SUNDAYS

NO whistling (but you can sing hymns out of tune)

NO peeling potatoes (but you can peel an orange, if you can find one)

NO reading rubbish (put Wicked Wales away, then)

NO cutting-out with a scissors (you'll have to use your teeth instead)

NO playing outside (but you can play at funerals – so put the canary in a box and bury it in the back garden)

IF YOU BREAK THESE REMARKABLE RULES YOU WILL NOT BE MAM'S PET!

THE HOPELESS BAND OF HOPE

Every Monday evening the children would return
to the chapel vestry to attend the hopeless Band of
Hope – to learn even more remarkable rules.
They had to swear an oath that they would never
touch a drop of alcohol. Then, they received a special
certificate:

CERTIFICATE

12 April 1888

I, JANE OWEN promise not to touch alcohol as
long as I shall live.

Signed   *Jane Owen*   Age: 6 years

I didn't touch alcohol – I only drank it! Hic!

CRAFTY CROOKS AND PAINFUL PUNISHMENTS

Many of the great-, great-, great-, great-grandfathers and grandmothers of the people who live in Australia today went out there from Wales during the Appalling Victorian Age. But they didn't win a fabulous raffle to go and live in a pleasant and sunny land. No, these were crafty crooks who were taken there in chains. Australia was to be their pathetic prison.

Many of the men were cruel criminals – murderers, terrorists, rioters and highwaymen – so they deserved to be punished painfully. But many of the women who were transported 15,000 miles away from Wales had done very little wrong.

What kind of judge would you be, do you think? Guess which punishment fitted which crime. (If you get this task wrong you will be transported to Australia – the land of sunny beaches and kangaroos):

Stealing a loaf of bread and some bacon is a very serious crime – you will be transported to Australia for 7 years.

No.	Name	Age	Where from?	Offence	Letter	Punishment
1.	Ellen Davies	19	Anglesey	stealing a loaf of bread and some bacon	A	transportation for 15 years
2.	Hanna Roberts	18	Holywell	murdering her husband with arsenic	B	transportation for 10 years
3.	Mary Jenkins	?	Monmouth	receiving stolen knives and forks	C	transportation for 7 years
4.	Fanny Bennett	13	Worthing, Sussex	stealing two shawls and an umbrella	D	to be hanged, then the sentence was changed to transportation for life
5.	Mary Davies	?	Merthyr Tydfil	a violent highway robber	E	transportation for 7 years

Answers: 1 and C; 2 and D; 3 and B; 4 and E; 5 and A.

It's obvious that many of the judges didn't believe in fair play. All they wanted was to send young women to Australia to be the wives and maids of the crafty male crooks. These were the Blind Dates of the Appalling Victorian Age.

UNLUCKY CABBAGES

Ruth Roberts of Bala was a very, very bad woman. She stole four cabbages from a garden in the town. And so, she was summoned to appear before her 'betters' in court:

Constable: I'm Bala's clever constable. I arrested Ruth Roberts for stealing the cabbages. To prove my case I have brought four cabbage stalks from the garden to court. You can see that the cabbage heads fit perfectly on these stalks.

Judge: Ruth Roberts, you are guilty of stealing cabbages. I am transporting you to be imprisoned in Van Diemen's Land (Australia) for seven years.

Ruth: (crying) Oh dear, I've made such a hotchpotch of everything!

If one of these ghastly girls had kept a diary,
she might have written about her experiences
like this:

Millbank, a fearsome prison in London
Tuesday 25 April 1848

Only one more nervous night to go now. Tomorrow
I sail to the end of the world to serve seven years as a
prisoner in Van Diemen's Land. I shall be 22 years
old, ugly and past it, when I return once more to dear
Swansea. And all I did was steal sixpence worth of
goods. This morning I saw what the nasty gaoler had
written about me:

Name:	Ann Thomas
From:	Swansea
Work:	Maid
Height:	4 foot 10 inches
Hair:	Dark brown
Eyes:	Light blue
Description:	Smallpox scars on her right cheek. A terrible temper.

Huh! Brown
hair indeed!
The gaoler has
shaved it all off!
Where will the
nits live now?

I'll show them what a really terrible temper is!

The Stately
Wednesday 15 November 1848

Seven long months at sea! This ship is soaking wet
and filthy. Several of the ghastly girl prisoners have

died already. We were given a new set of clothes for the journey – and most of us had been sentenced for stealing clothes in the first place! I'm fed up with having to sew quilts all day. I'd rather milk the cows on board ship and clean up after the pigs, the hens and the donkeys than sew. To tell you the truth, a few of us were so sick and tired of the work, we went on strike last week. Two of the girls were punished by being whipped on their bare backs with the cat-o'-nine-tails. But, because I was the leader, I received the most severe punishment. I was thrust into a wooden cask and made to stand in it for hours on end. I couldn't sit or lie down – it was so tiring. But I didn't show the captain how I felt. And then, I was given a bath – thrown into a dark, square hole, the grating closed on me and someone scrubbed my back with a scouring brush – like washing a sheep! Ow! I'd better keep my mouth shut from now on . . .

The Cascades Factory, Hobart, Van Diemen's Land
Friday 15 December 1853

And here we are – from one prison to another. The work is never-ending – washing and sewing, picking tar out of ropes, breaking up stones and, worst of all, having to stand in rows for the men to walk up and down to choose one of us as a wife. I feel like a cow in a market. Thank goodness, no one has chosen me yet. They've probably heard I've got a terrible temper.

But THEY can't break our spirits completely. The other day important visitors – Sir John Franklin, the Governor, and his wife – came to the factory with a very pompous clergyman called the Reverend Bedford. We all hate Bedford. And so, when he got up to speak, we girls got up at the same time, turned around, lifted our flimsy prison skirts and smacked our naked bottoms!

It was worth seeing the old fool's face turning bright purple! That'll teach the bumpkin a lesson!

Bottoms up, girls!

I've been in Australia for four years now. I shall be able to return to Wales a free woman in three years' time. Hip hip hurray!

OLD KING COAL

When Victoria was Queen, Coal was King (and he wasn't a merry old soul either).

Beyond Belief

Some of the fantastic facts about mining for coal and the super coal miners of the Appalling Victorian Age are almost beyond belief. What do you think – are they TRUE or FALSE?

1. In 1847 Charles Cliffe described the Rhondda like this:

The people of this pleasant valley depend almost entirely upon their animals . . . for their food. The air smells beautiful here – of wild flowers and mountain plants – and it's as quiet here as on a Sunday.

But in 1893 the Medical Officer of Health for the Rhondda had some very different and horrible comments to make about this lovely green valley:

There's a lot of human pee and poo, dung from the stables and sties, blood and the innards of animals from the slaughterhouses . . . the rotten corpses of cats and dogs; mangy old clothes and bedclothes and other rubbish in the river (Rhondda). The water is a filthy black colour. In warm weather the stench is unbearable.

TRUE *or* **FALSE**?

2. At the beginning of the Appalling Victorian Age, five- and six-year-old children had to work down the coal and iron mines – in the pitch dark, with water dripping down their necks and with only rats for company. In 1839, nine-year-old Jane Morgan slipped under the wheels of a dram and had to have her leg amputated. She never worked down the pit again.

Squeak, squeak! Why do all these children want to be my friends?

***TRUE* or *FALSE*?**

3. More and more coal miners dug tons upon tons of coal in Wicked Wales during the Appalling Victorian Age. Here are some starry statistics:

1874: 73,000 colliers produced 16.5 million tons of coal (that's a lot of coal)
1898: 127,000 colliers produced 36 million tons of coal (that's an awful lot of coal)
1908: 201,000 colliers produced 50 million tons of coal (that's an awful, awful lot of coal!)

If you were a star pupil you could make a brilliant graph of these figures and your hopeless history teacher would ask for your auto*graph*. But before that, are these statistics

***TRUE* or *FALSE*?**

4. As the colliers tramped together to work every morning and as they sauntered home from the pit at night they would sing horrendous hymns such as 'Guide Me, Oh Thou Great Jehovah' and stupid songs like 'The Green, Green Grass of Home', until the hills were alive with the sound of music.

TRUE or FALSE?

5. Pit ponies working underground were very clever. They knew how to steal water jacks from the colliers' pockets and they could chew tobacco better than their masters. But most importantly, they could sense danger – and help the coal miners by warning them.

TRUE or FALSE?

6. David Davies, Llandinam, became one of the most powerful pioneers of the south Wales coalfield. He tried to open a mine in the Rhondda, but after 15 months of digging, the colliers hadn't found any

sign of coal. On Saturday 3 March 1866 he told the
men to go home. All he had left in his pocket was
half a crown (12½p). The men said they'd like to have
his last half-crown. So he threw them the money.

But then, the men decided to work on for one
extra week without pay and EUREKA! On Friday
9 March they found a vein of excellent steam coal.
David Davies went on to establish the Ocean Coal
Company. He built new docks in Barry and he
became a very, very wealthy man – Wales's first
millionaire. But what about the colliers who helped
him, I wonder?

TRUE *or* FALSE?

7. The colliers were very happy working down the
pits for very little pay. They never moaned when
they had to work hard in atrocious conditions.

TRUE *or* FALSE?

8. Women loved working underground too. They
wore black overalls and did the same wearisome
work as the colliers.

TRUE *or* FALSE?

9. There were coal mines in Pembrokeshire,
Denbighshire and Flintshire during the Appalling
Victorian Age too. There were more colliers than
quarrymen in north Wales, but hideous historians
always seem to forget this fantastic fact.

TRUE *or* FALSE?

ANSWERS:

1. **True**, worst luck. So many people came to live in the Rhondda to work in the pits that the valley became overcrowded and their sewage and rubbish ended up in the river.

2. **True**. Some of the children had to pull trams underground with chains around their waists, like animals. In 1842 the government passed a law prohibiting children under ten from working underground. But some pitiless parents and heartless owners ignored the new law.

3. **Absolutely true**. Someone (but not the colliers of course) must have made a lot of money from all this coal.

4. **False** – there was no time to sing in the morning and they were too tired to sing at night.

5. **True** – honestly.

6. **True**. There are two statues to commemorate David Davies in Wales – one in Llandinam and one in Barry. They said that Margaret, his wondrous wife, could recite the whole of the New Testament by heart!

7. **False**. The colliers of south Wales loved going on strike and often refused to work unless they had better pay or working conditions. In 1898 half the coal mines in south Wales closed and 100,000 colliers went on strike for six months – no money, no clothes, no food. They starved, and eventually they had to go back to work without gaining ANYTHING. That's why they decided to join together to form one strong Union – the South Wales Miners' Federation (the Fed because they were so fed up with the owners).

I'm FED up with this strike!

8. **False**. After 1865 women were prohibited from working underground. But they continued to work on the surface, on the dirty, fiery and dangerous coal tips. To do this dirty job the women liked to dress up fashionably in fancy dresses and pretty bonnets, necklaces and brooches. Sometimes their cute dresses caught fire.

9. **True**, and in such places as Rhosllannerchrugog the colliers spoke very strange Welsh indeed: snowing wasn't *bwrw eira* but *odi*; to grasp something was *sbachu*; a small cake was called a *wicsen* and *nene* meant that (one).

Would you like to be a collier?

In that case you must enjoy:

- being filthy all the time
- working 12 hours a day
- going down into the earth's bowels in an open cage
- walking miles underground to get to the coalface
- kneeling or lying in narrow tunnels to cut coal
- washing in a tiny tin bath in front of the fire – with your wife scrubbing your back (Oops! Where's the soap?)
- coughing and coughing, because the coal dust has gone into your lungs.★

Do you still want to be a carefree collier? Go to see the doctor – there's something seriously wrong with you!

(★ The coal owners claimed that coal dust was good for the colliers! But, of course, they didn't want to have any themselves!)

Would you like to be a collier's wife?

In that case, find yourself a tidy miner – it will be difficult to recognise him once you're married, because every coal miner looks the same. You must enjoy:

- getting up at five in the morning to prepare his snap box (the fancy name for his lunch box)
- washing his filthy, sweaty clothes every week
- boiling water to help him wash in his tin bath in front of the fire (Oops! Here's the soap)
- scrubbing the house clean and free from coal dust every day

- trying to make sure you've got enough money to feed the family out of his tiny wage packet
- worrying endlessly that he's going to have an accident underground
- listening to him coughing and coughing all night
- bringing up a family of boys to be carefree colliers the same as their dad
- taking in other colliers as lodgers in your home – with all their dirty clothes and the filth from the pit – to help pay the rent.

And you still want to be a collier's wife? You might as well marry the pit! But at least you won't have to go out to work too!

I'm not sure which one of you is my darling Dai now!

APPALLING ACCIDENTS

Burning, drowning, choking, suffocating, being crushed – these are some of the ways colliers could be killed

underground in the Appalling Victorian Age. Accidents often happened because greedy owners were more concerned about making a huge profit than about the health and safety of their weary workers.

A FILE OF FASCINATING FACTS

Between 1868 and 1914 one collier was killed every six hours and 12 were injured every day.

Between 1850 and 1920 over 3,000 colliers were killed in the south Wales coalfield. This coalfield had the worst accident record in Britain.

In the Appalling Victorian Age's Guinness Book of Records the most atrocious accidents were:

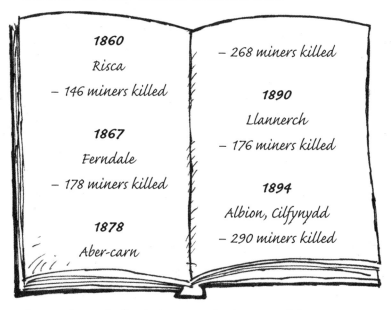

1860

Risca

– 146 miners killed

1867

Ferndale

– 178 miners killed

1878

Aber-carn

– 268 miners killed

1890

Llannerch

– 176 miners killed

1894

Albion, Cilfynydd

– 290 miners killed

It wasn't much fun being a coal miner, was it?

The Rhondda Shovel

(calling a shovel a shovel) 3 June, 1877 2d.

No Bravery Medal for Dodd

Scandal at Tynewydd!

Bet on Your Favourite Greyhound p.10
Perplexed Pigeons Panic p.2

A shocking scandal is rocking the Rhondda. Abby Dodd, one of the superheroes of the awful accident at Tynewydd Colliery, will not be receiving an Albert Medal for Bravery after all. But Queen Victoria will present the other four members of the rescue team with a medal each.

When we visited Abby Dodd he wasn't an 'appy man. 'I risked my life to save the lives of the five miners who were trapped underground by water in Tynewydd pit,' he told the correspondent of the *Rhondda Shovel*. 'A gang of us worked day and night for ten days to dig through the rock between us and the trapped men, but the rest of the gang were too afraid to cut through the last piece of rock. They realised, of course, that the air could rush out and the water rise up suddenly and drown us all. I'll be honest – I was shaking like a leaf too. We all knew what had happened to poor William Thomas, when he cut his way through rock to be rescued. The air had rushed out

and sucked William through. His head plugged the hole in the rock. He died instantly and it took us hours to release his head. He was only a young lad.' The brave collier's eyes filled with tears as he related this terrible tale.

Is it surprising that Abby Dodd is angry and un'appy? HE was the first member of the rescue team to venture into the hole where the five men were trapped. HE was the one who helped them to get out.

We questioned the pit owner about this shocking scandal but all he would say was, 'Are you surprised he isn't getting the Albert Medal? That man has made my life a misery ever since the accident. He says that I was to blame – that I hadn't checked the water that was escaping from another pit into this one. Abby Dodd has been a nasty nuisance – he doesn't deserve a Medal!'

But the pit owner wouldn't tell us where he was during the rescue effort.

More about this exclusive story next week.

96

STRANGE SUPERSTITIONS

Colliers had to be very brave to venture underground where they could be poisoned by gas, crushed by a roof fall or killed in an explosion. This is why they believed in strange superstitions and followed their own strange rules, so that they could recognise weird warnings down the pit.

Ridiculous Rules

To be a lucky miner, remember:
- if you have forgotten your snap box (the miner's special name for his lunch box) don't go back for it or bad luck will follow (surely it would be worse to starve all day)
- don't whistle underground (especially out of tune)
- you should only wash your back ONCE a week – or you'll be the weakest link.

I told you not to wash your back too often!

Weird Warnings

Be very careful if you see:
- a woman on the way to work – bad luck will follow
- a woman underground – there will be a disaster
- a bird hovering around the pithead – one miner said he saw a robin hovering around the pithead before a major disaster in Llanbradach in 1901. (Why didn't he mention this BEFORE the disaster?)
- a white mouse underground (how on earth could it remain white down a coal mine?)
- rats disappearing – a disaster will follow, and there'll be no one to share your sandwiches and Welsh cakes (if you've remembered your snap box, of course).

And many coal miners believed they could hear the sound of ghosts tapping underground. These were the KNOCKERS, who knocked and knocked in the night. Ooh . . . Ooh . . . Ooh . . .

Knock, knock, who's there?

Mr and Mrs Knocker Ooh . . . Ooh . . . Ooh . . .

BAA-R-BAA-ROUS SHEEP

Shameless sheep were a nuisance in the south Wales valleys. Flocks of mangy blaa-ck sheep came down from the baa-ck of beyond, baa-ttering down hedges, fences and gates, gobbling up every plant, every tree and flower and scoffing the tasty vegetables in the miners' gardens. What a baa-nquet! Some sheep were so baa-r-baa-rous, they even stole baa-ra brith, and baa-nanas from the houses, and one or two had a baa-th and baa-rbecue before going home.

WHAT'S IN A NAME?

There were lots and lots of men called Tom, Dick and Dai living higgledy-piggledy on top of one another in the south Wales valleys during the Appalling Victorian Age. And with sad surnames, such as Jones, Davies and Evans, it was hard to tell one Tom, Dick or Dai from another. So they gave them nice nicknames.

Ask your friends (Bill and Ben) to guess the meanings of these cool nicknames:

1. Dai Sosban:

(A) he sold saucepans
(B) he came from Llanelli – the centre for saucepan-making
(C) he sang '*Sosban Fach*' all the time.

2. Johnny Lap:

(A) he liked to eat *teisen lap* (a special cake popular with miners in their snap boxes)
(B) he didn't stop talking (yap, yap)
(C) he liked to sit in his wife's lap.

3. Dai Small Coal:

(A) he only dug small pieces of coal from the coalface
(B) he ate small pieces of coal for his supper
(C) he put small coal on the fire every night to keep it alive.

4. Evans Above:

(A) he was the village preacher
(B) he lived above his butcher's shop
(C) he worked on the surface of the coal mine.

5. Dick Full Pelt:

(A) he did everything at a very quick pace

(B) he wore a fur coat to work (a 'pelt' is an animal skin)

(C) he was full of himself.

Can't you guess the answers, Ned No Answers and Johnny Joker? Go to the corner and stand on a stool with your dunce's cap on. Here they are:

4A (Heavens Above!); 5A
1B; 2B; 3C;

As you have probably noticed, many of the Appalling Victorians living in the wicked Welsh valleys had learned a bit of English, and spoke Wenglish (Welsh/English) like this:

> 'I am a little collier
> Working under groun';
> The *rhaff* will never *torri*
> When I go up and down,
> *Bwyd* when I am hungry,
> *Cwrw* when I'm dry,
> *Gwely* when I'm *blino*,
> *Nefoedd* when I die!'

CLEVER CLUES

TO UNDERSTAND THIS WOEFUL WENGLISH, YOU'LL NEED TO KNOW SOME REAL WELSH WORDS: *RHAFF* = 'ROPE'; *TORRI* = 'BREAK'; *BWYD* = 'FOOD'; *CWRW* = 'BEER'; *GWELY* = 'BED'; *BLINO* = 'TIRED'; *NEFOEDD* = 'HEAVEN'.

THE GLORIOUS GORSEDD OF THE BARDS

Would you like to join the Gorsedd of the Bards in the Appalling Victorian Age? In that case, you should:

1. Wear a comical costume
2. Learn the Bardic Alphabet
3. Write pathetic poems
4. Choose a natty pen name
5. Do everything in Welsh.

1. Wear a comical costume

The Gorsedd costume changed several times during the Appalling Victorian Age, according to the latest fashion.

The fashion before 1850:
✠ bare head
✠ a white, blue or green armband to show which order of bards you belong to
✠ bare feet

The fashion around 1894:
✠ a black beret (like Johnny Onions)
✠ a white, blue or green sash
✠ war medals (Is There Peace? *A Oes Heddwch?*)
✠ a pretty little white apron
✠ tidy shoes

The fussy fashion from 1894 until now:

✚ a crazy Celtic headdress
✚ a long white, blue or green nightgown
✚ white wellingtons in case of mud and rain (then they'll go black) – the latest twenty-first century fashion.

2. Learn the Bardic Alphabet

This was a clever alphabet invented by Iolo Morganwg, the father of the Gorsedd. He claimed that it was the old alphabet used by the Celtic Druids back in the Iron Age. This was all lies, of course, but as always (well, almost) everyone believed Iolo's lies.

Some dodgy druids chose to have this Bardic Alphabet carved on their gravestones – but then, no one could be sure who'd been buried where!

Do you remember who was buried here?

Give us a clue.

3. Write pathetic poems

What on earth is this 'poet' trying to say?

> *The Resurrection's mysteries*
> *In Nature's plans abide,*
> *Lo, life from death resurgent*
> *Is everywhere descried.*

No idea? And there were 3,000 similar, profound lines in this GREAT poem by Ieuan Glan Geirionnydd. He won a prize for this rubbish in an eisteddfod in Rhuddlan in 1850.

But the worst 'poet' of all was John Evans – the Cockle Bard (he sold cockles). His friends gave him the tantalising title 'The Princely Cockling Archdruid' (doesn't it warm the cockles of your heart?) and they dressed him up in a blue coat and hat, with a crown of colourful beads to go to eisteddfodau. Everyone applauded him when he got up on the stage and recited his GREAT poem:

> *Eisteddfod bards, you rule!*
> *Your poems are so cool,*
> *They make me look a fool.*
> *Eisteddfod bards, you rule!*

The Cockle Bard came from Menai Bridge, Anglesey, and when the Britannia Railway Bridge was built across the Menai Strait by Robert Stephenson in the 1840s, he 'composed' his famous comic poem to the four stone lions which guard it:

> *Four lions bald,*
> *Four lions fat,*
> *Two on this side*
> *And two on that.*

And this is how he 'sang' to the monument built to the
'Marquis of Anglesey' at Llanfair Pwllgwyngyll,
Anglesey. The unfortunate Marquis had lost one leg in
the great battle of Waterloo:

> *Marquis of Anglesey,*
> *By everyone adored,*
> *With your hand on your sword,*
> *Don't you get bored?*

Brill! The Cockle Bard thought he was such a fantastic
poet, he decided to ask Her Highness Queen Victoria
to marry him. Perhaps his letter to her went something
like this:

> *Dearest Vic,*
> *You're so chic,*
> *Please marry me,*
> *Oh, marry me quick.*

And she might have answered:

> *Dear Cockle Bard,*
> *You're trying too hard,*
> *Remember Vic*
> *Is not your chick!*

4. Choose a natty pen name

To be one of THE great poets in the Gorsedd of the Bards you had to have a truly natty bardic pen name like these:

MAM O NEDD (Winifred Coombe-Tennant – the only mother from Neath!)
DEWI DAWEL (*Dawel* = *tawel* = quiet – Ssh! in case he wakes up!)
IORWERTH GOES HIR (LONG-LEGGED EDWARD – pull the other one!)
HWFA MÔN (not the hoover of Anglesey – hoovers hadn't been invented yet!)
GWENRHIAN GWYNEDD (at least it was better than her real name – Fanny Mary Katherine Bulkeley-Owen)

If you want a clean island, ask for Hwfa Môn!

5. Do everything in Welsh

And fair play to the bards and the druids, they did do everything in Welsh when almost all the other Appalling Victorians in Wicked Wales thought it was cool and fashionable to speak English and to let the Welsh language die. But not everyone wanted to be a Druid or a Bard in the glorious Gorsedd of the Bards. They had to use brute force to make poor old Thomas Gee, the editor of *Baner ac Amserau Cymru*, the most important Welsh newspaper of the time, join them.

Thomas Gee: No, no, I don't want to be a Druid. NO . . . Arrrgh!

Archdruid Clwydfardd: I'll drag you into the circle myself if I have to.

Thomas Gee: Stop, stop!

Archdruid Clwydfardd: Stand there. You've got to be a Druid.

Thomas Gee: Oh, OK then! Gee! . . . thanks.

THE BARDS' BRILLIANT BOSS

The grumpy gang of bards, druids, and ovates (second-class druids) in the Gorsedd of the Bards had to have a brilliant boss to keep them in order. And so they had a fantastic idea. What about having an ARCHdruid? – a joyous job because you could wear a golden crown, a breastplate around your neck and a cream nightie.

I wonder why that Archdruid is called Clwydfardd? Is it because he always sits on the fence?

clues:
clwyd = gate
fardd = *bardd* = bard

Clwydfardd (or David Griffiths as his Mam called him) was the first Archdruid of Wales. He was dead beat when he began the job because he was already 88 years old.

Hwfa Môn was the first Archdruid to dress glamorously. They put his picture on souvenirs: *A Present from Wicked Wales.*

Hwfa Môn
Father of Wales

One important ceremony the Archdruid has to perform is to ask the Gorsedd and the audience in important ceremonies, '*A Oes Heddwch?*' (Is there Peace?). This question must be asked three times (perhaps everyone is so old that they can't remember they've answered it twice already!).

And what does the Archdruid use to perform this peaceful Peace Ceremony? A sword of course! – a huge sword which could chop the heads off ten people at once! Thank goodness the Keeper of the Sword is a hunk of a man who knows what he's doing.

BARMY OR BRAVE? THAT IS THE QUESTION

In 1865 some weary Welsh people were fed up of being poor and miserable in Wales, so they decided to travel 7,000 miles across the ocean to live in another, even poorer and more miserable country. Barmy or brave?

Perhaps they hadn't been told the whole truth and nothing but the truth before they ventured out . . .

The Mimosa
30 June 1865

Dear Taid and Nain,
Hurray! We've almost reached paradise. I'm sick and tired of this ship – no room to run and play, biscuits full of maggots and babies screaming all the time. And then there are terrible storms and the passengers are seasick over everything. (Maggots don't look as tasty when you see them for the second time!) But we'll be in Patagonia soon – a land full of cattle and sheep, and fruit, such as apples, gooseberries and currants (mmm . . . oh for an apple tart). And no more rain or showers as we're used to in Blaenau Ffestiniog. I don't suppose I shall ever see you again, Taid and Nain, but I'll write to tell you all about paradise.
Your excited grandson, William

Hoi! Don't eat me – I want to see paradise too, remember!

Dear Taid and Nain,

Help! I don't know why Mam and Dad brought me out to this awful country. We have been living in this cave for a month and it's incredibly hot here. Oh how I would love to see some of Blaenau's rain now! The land is as dry as a bone and there aren't any tame cattle or sheep here – only evil eagles, horrible ostriches and guanacos – a vicious type of sheep. One of the settlers went out to try and milk one of the wild cows yesterday. He hung onto its tail, but the cow dragged him through the sand and thorns until its tail broke off in his hands. Everyone here is fed up of this cruel country.

Your tearful grandson,
William

PS They've decided to call this country the *Wladfa* (the Colony – how original!) – the Dump would have been a better name.

Dyffryn Camwy
24 December 1865

Dear Taid and Nain,

Help! Help! Things are going from bad to worse. We're (almost) starving. My mouth has turned green, as I have to graze grass for food. I shall turn into a sheep soon. Ba-aa! One of the men ate a fox last week. Our leader's name is Edwin Roberts and he says that the Government of Argentina is going to give us a lot of land and money to settle here properly. And he insists on hoisting the Welsh banner here every morning. Then the Argentinian soldiers come along and hoist their blue-and-white banner and claim that this is their land, not ours, and that we must learn to speak Spanish, not Welsh!

To cap it all, ferocious Indians live nearby. We're expecting them to attack us at any moment. They're angry because we've taken their land (actually, I can see their point). Perhaps they'll scalp us . . . Help!

Your (frightened out of his wits)
grandson, W . . . W . . . William

LIVING HISTORY – IN A WOEFUL WORKHOUSE

One fate you should avoid like the plague in your horrible history lessons is taking part in a 'Living History' experience (a completely crazy idea thought up by cool and over-enthusiastic history teachers – every actual Appalling Victorian is as dead as a dodo, of course). But you can foil your teacher's plans by offering to organise your own brilliant Living History lesson. And the most horrendous and horrible of all such sessions would be Living History in a woeful workhouse. Try to persuade a few other hopeless teachers to join in as well.

1. The first thing you need to do is to separate the men from the women. When families entered a workhouse in the old days, the men had to go to one part of the building, women to another, boys to another, and girls to another. And they weren't allowed to see one another until they left the workhouse – maybe forever and ever. Amen.

2. Then you must dress your teachers like the penniless poor. Remember to scrub them well from head to toe to get rid of any fleas or head lice. Dress the women in long, shapeless dresses made of hard, rough material and the men in scratchy shirts with pieces of cord to hold their trousers up and tie their trouser legs under the knee. Their footwear should be wooden clogs.

Would you like the latest penniless poor haircut today, madam?

3. You will really enjoy preparing the food for the woeful workhouse inmates:
Gruel (oatmeal and water – like thin porridge)
Bread and cheese (if they're very lucky)
Water.

They won't need knives, forks or spoons. They can eat the gruel with their hands! Sometimes the poor would be allowed a little meat, *cawl* or fish, such as a herring, or even potatoes. But the most important fact of all is that workhouse food was very monotonous. Some of the poorest people were so desperate for food that they ate ground animal bones (try this on your teachers!).

4. If your teachers look pale and drawn after a day of acting Living History scenes in the woeful workhouse, you can bring the bloom back into their cheeks. Make them stand on their heads for half an hour at a time. Or give them a good slap across the face. This should make their cheeks look flushed and rosy!

5. And to top it all you can allocate boring and horrible tasks to all the teachers to keep them busy. They should get up at five in the morning. Then, the women should wash, iron, scrub the floors and pick oakum (clean ropes full of tar) until their hands are blistered and their fingers are bleeding. The men will have to smash large stones into tiny pieces which can fit through minute holes in a grill. (But perhaps even this is better than trying to teach mathematics or geography to extremely dim pupils like you.)

6. And if the teachers misbehave, they will have to be punished (only for the sake of the Living History session, of course!).

In the workhouse in Forden, Powys, Mary Reynal was whipped in public for stealing food. Mary Davies was locked into a scold's bridle (a metal frame which was put around her head with a metal tongue to go into her mouth) for making too much noise in the poorhouse. But be careful – don't punish them too harshly. After all, you want good marks in your next history test!

This could be very useful for a nagging teacher.

After this absolutely amazing session, and with a bit of good luck, your history teachers won't mention the weary words 'Living History' ever again.

QUARRELSOME QUARRYMEN

During the Appalling Victorian Age slates from Wicked Wales were used to roof houses throughout the world. But between 1900 and 1903 a huge dispute broke out between George Sholto Gordon Douglas-Pennant, Baron Penrhyn (*1) and his 2,800 workmen in Penrhyn Quarry (*2).

ONE against 2,800 – no contest? And no hope for the brutal Baron? What do you think?

(★1) Baron Penrhyn was so high and mighty, he deserves a nasty little ditty sung to him:

The Noble Baron Penrhyn,
He had three thousand men,
(well, 2,800 actually)
In his quarry of slate
He locked the gate
To prove he was BOSS again.

(★2) Penrhyn Quarry was the largest man-made hole in the world. They said you could see it from the moon. (How on earth did they know? Perhaps the man in the moon had sent them a picture postcard!)

Let's join in the battle between them. This is the kind of letter Baron Penrhyn wrote to the quarrymen:

20 November 1900
Penrhyn Castle

You men must obey ME. You can't tell me how to run my quarry. You can't join a Union to force me to give you better pay and holidays. I'm the boss here and I'm going to lock you out of the quarry to teach you a very hard lesson, you disgraceful workmen.

William Jones's letter on behalf of the 2,800 quarrymen:

22 November 1900
Stryd Fawr, Bethesda

Huh! We're going to go on strike. We've had a gutsful of you and your spiteful steward, Mr Young. We're going to unite in a Union to try to improve our lives (*3).

(*3) According to the doctors in the quarry, the quarrymen's health was poor because they never had a proper bath (PONG!). And they drank too much tea – tea for breakfast, tea for dinner, tea for tea and tea for supper – and that tea had been stewing in the teapot for hours. But perhaps tea helped to clear the lethal slate dust from their lungs.

What's for tea, Mari fach?

Tea, of course!

We've discussed this in the *Caban* (*4). We won't return to this hole until you, Baron Penrhyn, listen to us. United we stand!

(*4) Every dinner time the sweaty quarrymen squashed into the *Caban* in the quarry (*ych-a-fi* – just think of the sweat and stench!). They would choose a Chairman to keep order.

Cabin Rules

Every quarryman must be addressed as 'Brother'

No spitting

No swearing

No playing cards

Discussion topics for this month:

1. Sunday sermons
2. The charismatic career of David Lloyd George MP
3. Who is the best dressed – the collier or the quarryman?
4. Who is happier – Baron Penrhyn in his castle or a quarryman in his smallholding? No mention of rugby or football.

(Thank goodness dinner time only lasted half an hour!)
But the quarrymen enjoyed the odd (very odd!) joke too.

JOKE 1:

Quarryman 1: What have you *been* up to today?
Quarryman 2: Putting smoke into sacks! (Ha! Ha!)

JOKE 2:

Quarryman 1: What do you find in an empty house?
Quarryman 2: Plenty of room!

I hope you didn't die of laughter!

Baron Penrhyn:

June 1901

Quarrelsome quarrymen – I'm willing to pay every man who returns to work in Penrhyn Quarry £1 each, at once. Forget the strike – and you will have £1 in your pocket. Come along!

Wili Jones:

June 1901

No way! Perhaps 500 of the strikers have been foolish enough to return to work – but I shall NEVER break the strike and be a shameful *cynffonnwr* (*5). I've put a notice in the window of my home saying 'NO SCABS IN THIS HOUSE!' (*6)

(*5) They called the men who broke the strike *cynffonwyr* (men with tails); not because they had grown tails but because they were like dogs wagging their tails to please the steward and the Baron.

(*6) But perhaps the scabs had to go back to work – with no pay, no money, no food and their wives and children dying of hunger. Scabs? Or wise, responsible men?

My Lord:

1903

Haven't you had enough yet? You all, and your wives and children too, look so poor. Why don't you follow your friends and look for work in the south Wales coal mines, or go to America? Thank goodness, some of the men are wiser than you lot and they've returned to work. You shouldn't attack them and shout nasty names at them. The police and the soldiers have shown you that there's no point rioting and attacking me or my wonderful workers (*7).

(★7) The quarrelsome quarrymen deserve to be celebrated in song too:

> *The quarrymen fought so hard*
> *To keep the strike on track.*
> *They hated the Baron's £1 a head,*
> *His bribe to send them back.*
> *Scabs! Scabs! Scabs!*

The *cynffonwyr* were mercilessly hounded out of chapels and villages like Sling and Tregarth. These very bad feelings persisted for years and years – long after the end of the strike.

That's what happens to a scab from Sling!

W. Jones:

January 1904

Please, dear Baron Penrhyn, may I have my job in the quarry back? The great strike came to an end last November and I'm still unemployed. My family is dying of hunger. Please forgive my past comments.

Baron Penrhyn:

1904

No chance. Because of the great strike there is less demand for slates now and you, quarrelsome quarrymen, are to blame. I'll be fine because I own thousands of hectares of farmland (*8) and a magnificent home in Penrhyn Castle.

> THE SCORE FOR THE GREAT PENRHYN STRIKE
> Baron Penrhyn: 1
> 2,800 quarrymen: 0 (nil)

(*8) Baron Penrhyn owned huge estates – over 29,000 hectares altogether, with 618 farms and 873 cottages. The family made its huge fortune by forcing slaves to work for them for nothing on their enormous sugar plantations in Jamaica – shocking!!!

But in 1949 the family gave the Castle to the National Trust and now everyone can visit it (ha ha, Georgie). By 1964, the McAlpine company was running the quarry (serve you right, Baron High and Mighty!).

A GALLERY OF COOL CHARACTERS

Here are some of the coolest characters who lived during the Appalling Victorian Age:

Dr William Price, Llantrisant – the colourful Doctor

The Appalling Victorians of Wicked Wales didn't know what to make of the colourful Doctor Price of Llantrisant. But they did know that he was a very funny-peculiar man! His scintillating story reads like a soap opera:

What was he – a superhero or a crazy crank?

This is the evidence:

1. He was a good doctor. He didn't accept payment from the poor. He tried to transplant a piece of bone (he was a hundred years before his time) but he failed and the patient died (a very unfortunate experiment).

2. He was a vegetarian (eating cabbages, peas, beans . . . no bacon, rabbit or chicken).

3. He hated smoking and refused to treat patients who smoked. Once, on a train from Merthyr to Pontypridd, he asked a man who was smoking a pipe to extinguish it.

I wonder why people think I'm odd?

The man refused. The Doctor snatched the pipe and threw it out of the window. Then, he threatened the man he would throw him out too if he complained.

4. He was one of the challenging Chartists (more about them on page 31) – who believed that every man should have the vote! After the Newport rising he escaped to France dressed as a woman!

5. He liked to walk the hills around Pontypridd stark naked – what a shock for the sheep! He never wore socks because he believed they were unhygienic.

6. He said he was a druid in the Gorsedd of the Bards. He would hold strange ceremonies on the Rocking Stone on Pontypridd Common. As a druid, he wore a colourful costume – a white cloak, red waistcoat and green trousers (like Mr Urdd!). On his head he wore a large hat of fox skin with the fox's legs and

Thank goodness my beard and hair are long enough to cover my bits and pieces!

tail hanging down over his shoulders. He never cut
his hair, and when he was old he had two long plaits
hanging down his back (he was one of the Happy
Hippies of Welsh History).

The Climax

When the colourful Doctor was 84 years old he had
a 28-year-old girlfriend called Gwenllian Llywelyn
and they had two children – Jesus Christ the Second
(he didn't believe in the first one) and Penelope. When
Jesus Christ II was five months old he died. The Doctor
decided to burn his son's body, not to bury it, as every
other respectable Appalling Victorian did. He cremated
the body on farmland near his home. Local people saw
the fire and rushed to rescue the body. Dr Price was
taken to court:

Dr William Price: I've got every right, Lord
Judge, to cremate my own son's body. I'm not
breaking the law. I believe burying the dead is a
dangerous and dirty custom . . .

The Judge: Mm . . . very interesting,
Doctor. No, you haven't broken the law, so you can
have Jesus Christ II's body back, to cremate it.
The Doctor is not guilty. Release him.

And of course, when the doctor himself died at
93 years old in 1893, he had arranged the whole
ceremony. His body was burned on a great bonfire –
the first time such a ritual had been seen in Wales.

Thousands bought tickets to see the show! And every pub in the district ran dry.

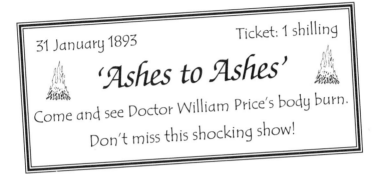

31 January 1893   Ticket: 1 shilling

'Ashes to Ashes'

Come and see Doctor William Price's body burn.

Don't miss this shocking show!

If Dr Price lived today people would think he was perfectly normal. Perhaps he is Llan**TRI**sant's fourth saint.

In Wales, we should celebrate Dr Price's Night not Guy Fawkes Night!

Dic Aberdaron (Richard Robert Jones) – the Talented Tramp

He only just makes it into the Appalling Victorian Age because Dic died in 1843. Guess where he was from?! But he preferred to roam the countryside as a hopeless (and probably smelly) hobo than stay at home in Aberdaron.

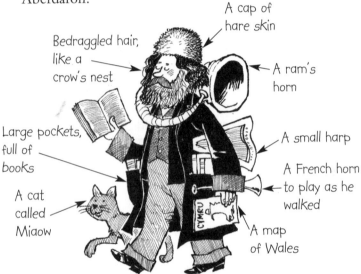

A cap of hare skin

Bedraggled hair, like a crow's nest

A ram's horn

Large pockets, full of books

A small harp

A French horn to play as he walked

A cat called Miaow

A map of Wales

But what else made Dic so cool? People said he could speak 35 languages although he had never been to school. (Tell your German and French teachers this – they'll have a fit.) But when they listed the languages, Holish-German, Holish-Dutch (or Double Dutch?) and Yiddish were on the list! And yet, perhaps he COULD speak 14 languages – Latin, Greek, Welsh, English . . . When someone asked the man himself, 'How many languages can you speak, Dic?' his smart answer was, 'Only one at a time!' Dic was a really cool character. And he was famous for one (or two!) other things as well:

'Letting off two farts at once was one of Dic's tricks, One for half a crown and one for seven and six!'

(Historical clue – half a crown was worth about 12½ pence. Seven and six was three times as much.)

Betsi Cadwaladr (Elizabeth Davies) – The Lady without a lamp

Every history book about the Appalling Victorian Age writes adoringly about Florence Nightingale, the notable nurse, because she cared for the seriously wounded soldiers of the Crimean War. Betsi Cadwaladr from Bala knew the 'Lady with the Lamp' well, and her recollections of fussy Florence aren't quite as flattering.

But was Betsi telling the truth? In her autobiography she recalls all kinds of bizarre adventures she experienced as she travelled the world:

◆ hunting kangaroos in Australia
◆ tying up a Portuguese man with a rope and throwing him into the sea three times in Rio de Janeiro – to teach him a lesson (or two or three!)
◆ and acting 'Lady Macbeth' on board ship in Calcutta!

But these adventures don't compare with the drama that took place between Betsi and Florence.

BETSI: We've come all the way out here to Scutari to nurse sick soldiers. They're dying like flies in this dirty, horrible hospital.

FLO: We don't need your help here. Go and mend the soldiers' clothes. Get out of the way of the real nurses. You're too old to be a nurse. (Well, Betsi was 75 years old!)

BETSI: I've had a gutsful (well, not quite) of this awful food – we only have leftovers from the patients' meals. While you, Miss High-and-mighty Nightingale, have three-course meals cooked by a French chef every day.

FLO: But I'm an important lady. You watch your tongue, Betsi.

BETSI: Do you think I'm a dog or an animal? I don't like you, Miss Nightingale. I'm going to go to Balaclava (a place, not a hat), to nurse the wounded there.

FLO: Good riddance to bad rubbish, you cheeky old Welsh woman!

TRUE or **FALSE**?

True, probably, because even horrendous historians admit that Florence Nightingale was a headstrong and haughty woman (perhaps that's why she was so successful as a nurse at the time!).

A QUIZ ABOUT MORE COOL CHARACTERS

How many of these cool characters from the Appalling Victorian Age can you name? How many do your history teachers know? Keep the score so that you know what kind of teachers they really are (the marks are with the answers).

1. *I was born in the town of Merthyr,*
    And became a famous composer,
    My 'Myfanwy' so brill
    Gave choirs a thrill,
    So they made me a music professor.

    ★   ★   ★

2. *John Rowlands from Denbigh, that's me.*
    My childhood was poor as could be.
    The workhouse was tough
    And they treated me rough
    So I scarpered and went off to sea.

    Later, I altered my name
    And as Livingstone's finder won fame.
    But despite my success
    I'm a brute, I confess,
    For I treated the natives with shame.

    ★   ★   ★

3. *Welsh costume I loved to invent,*
    With a bed-gown and shawl like a tent.
    So in tall hat and pinny,
    If you feel like a ninny,
    Put the blame on Gwenynen Gwent.

In Westminster borough you'll see
A clock that's more famous than me.
   Though I was quite small
   My husband was tall,
And a builder of note, you'll agree.

*   *   *

4. I took a long trip from Cyfarthfa
    And went to make iron in Russia.
       The ironworks thrived,
       The workers survived,
    In a twll of a town called Hughes-ovka.

*   *   *

5. Near Swansea I snapped with a lens,
    All my wealthy relations and friends.
       In my mansion so fine
       I had plenty of time
    To explore all the latest trends.

COUNT THE SCORES:

1-10: A useless teacher, go back to sleep.
11-20: A promising teacher, but there's room for improvement.
21-26: An excellent teacher: you should swallow everything you hear without question.

ANSWERS

1. Joseph Parry (1841–1903) – a composer and professor of music at Aberystwyth University College. Male voice choirs love singing his sentimental song 'Myfanwy' and shedding tears of *hiraeth*. Joe's home in 4 Chapel Row, Merthyr, is a museum today – but don't tell your teachers in case they organise a boring field trip to see it.
SCORE: 4 marks

2. H.M. Stanley (1841–1904) – the best-known Welshman in the world after he came across Dr Livingstone, the important missionary, lost in Ujiji in Africa in 1871. Stan the Man hated Wales because he had had such a chilling childhood in Denbigh. He said very nasty things about the place. But he wasn't such a saint himself. He was extremely cruel to the natives of the Congo in Africa. He whipped them – 300 strokes a time.
SCORE: 4 marks

3. Augusta Hall (1802–1896) – the Lady of Llanover Hall near Newport. She fell head over heels in love with everything Welsh and promoted local *eisteddfodau*, folk singing and playing the triple harp.

And she invented the Welsh Costume – with its prickly flannel skirt, its bumptious bed-gown and really ugly tall black hat. And that is why Welsh girls have to dress up so stupidly every St David's Day. Because Augusta buzzed around so much, fussing and bustling all the time, she was called the 'Bee of Gwent' (but at least she wasn't a <u>Bum</u>ble Bee). Bee's husband: Sir Ben(jamin) Hall (1802–1867) installed 'Big Ben' in its clock tower in London. Buzz off, Bee and Ben! *SCORE: 4 marks each*

4. John Hughes (1814–1889) – from Cyfarthfa, Merthyr Tydfil (once again!). The Tsar of Russia invited him to open ironworks and coal mines in Russia. He established the town of Hughes-ovka (Yuzovka in Russian) and by 1889, 20,000 people lived there – many of them in horrible hovels, even worse than those in Merthyr. The air was black and the horses, dogs and cats were grey with soot. Today the town is called Donetsk and everyone has long forgotten about Mr Hughes of Cyfarthfa. *SCORE: 6 marks*

They had to change the name. Hughes-ovka was so difficult to say.

5. John Dillwyn Llewelyn (1810–1880) who lived in a mansion in Penllergaer near Swansea was one of the best photographers in the world! He was related to Fox Talbot, who invented photography. He liked taking pictures of his wealthy family, and plants, but not of the ordinary people of Swansea in the Appalling Victorian Age unfortunately. Now that would have been really useful for useless historians. *SCORE: 6 marks*

FUN AND GAMES

By the end of the Appalling Victorian Age watching tedious teams and idiotic individuals playing all kinds of sports had become one of the favourite hobbies of Wicked Wales (among the men, at least; the women were too busy working – or gossiping!).

Seven Silly Stories about Rugby

Although the Welsh Rugby Union was founded in Neath in 1881, it took them years to get used to the egg-shaped ball.

In 1881 Wales lost to England by 7 goals, 1 drop goal and 13 tries to NIL (0!) – and Wales was lucky to score nothing! And when Ireland played Wales in 1884, Ireland were two players short, so they borrowed two Welsh players! Who won? Who cares!

Some players were brave, or stupid. J. Conway Rees, the Cardiff centre, broke his collarbone at the beginning of the game against England in 1893. But he played on to the bitter end with just one arm – and helped to score the winning try!

Teams would play underhand tricks on one another. When Llanelli played against Lampeter College, the students used to prepare a great feast before the game (but they didn't eat any of it themselves!). For the first half of the game the Llanelli players couldn't concentrate on anything except breaking wind!

Some of the teams dressed strangely. Appalling Victorian teams didn't have special colours, so one team would wear caps during the game so that they could recognize their fellow players. The Llanelli fullback was so cold in one match that he wore his overcoat throughout the game and yet he managed to tackle and kick the ball well. In Cardiff some players wore bowler hats. This is how a rugby player might have dressed in the 1880s:

'Tam o' Shanter' cap with a tassel hanging down

High-necked shirt

Long sleeves

Welsh woollen stockings

Tight trousers

Hob-nailed boots (Ouch!)

Red handkerchief in which to carry kit

When Llanelli Rugby Club was established they played in dark blue colours. Then they changed to shirts with quarters of primrose yellow and rose pink. (Wow! – How very pretty!). They turned Scarlet in 1884.

The early referees were really hopeless and they were treated badly. The home crowd would become very angry if its team didn't win and would throw mud and stones at the referees (BANG! SMASH!). When one team was playing very badly the other team would wind the opposition up by sending them cards like these:

In loving memory of the
Cardiff Rugby Team
who fell asleep on the Gloucester rugby ground
28 November 1891
'Not dead, just resting!'

The best Welsh player during the Appalling Victorian Age was Arnold Gould, of Newport and Wales. They used to say that Wales 'was bound to win by one Goul(d) to nil when he played' (a rubbishy rugby joke!).

When the game was very boring Evan and David James, two brothers who played for Swansea, used to fool around to entertain the crowd. They would walk on their hands from the touchline all the way to the goalpost!

We should go to play in Australia!

Five pointless points about football

When Wales began playing international football games, the scores were much higher than they are today (thank goodness!). Wales lost to Scotland by 9 goals to nil in 1878 but beat Ireland by 11 goals to nil in 1888. Then, in 1896, England defeated Wales by 9 goals to 1.

Wrexham Football Club was established in 1872, but in the beginning they would have been odd 'Robins' because they played in blue and white. And in the early games they fielded 15 or 16 players, who all wanted the ball at the same time. It was shambolic!

One of the surprising stars who played for Wrexham and Wales was Arthur Lea. He only had one arm! Yet somehow he was a talented cricketer too. What a star!

Another starry star was the gifted goalkeeper Leigh Richmond-Roose. He was SO superstitious! He always wore the same unwashed shorts and under them, a pair of very fishy, filthy pants. He liked to come out of his goal to stand in the centre of the pitch in the middle of a game. He could thump a ball with his fist halfway up the field. If the game was boring he would lean on a goalpost and chat to the crowd. What a cool character!

Wales's superstar was the midfielder Billy Meredith. He played for both Manchester United and Manchester City and won 48 caps for Wales. His schoolteacher taught Meredith how to kick a ball accurately. He would place a penny on the ground in the schoolyard, and if Billy could land the ball on the penny he was allowed to keep it. You could suggest this to your PE teacher, but do make sure that he uses £20 notes instead of pennies!

Stunning Cyclists

Towards the end of the Appalling Victorian Age four stunning cyclists lived in the Aberaman/Aberdare areas of Wicked Wales:

Arthur Linton
Tim Linton
Samuel Linton
(OK, OK, they were three brothers – you must be a genius!)
and Jimmy Michael.

It's not easy playing in all these caps!

All four were World Champions! Sometimes Arthur, Tim and Jimmy rode together on one long bike. Can you imagine how fast they could go?

Shall we go round the world today, boys?

Arthur Linton won a very important race from Bordeaux to Paris in 1896. But ... he died two months later at only 24 years old. Doctors now believe that this ambitious cyclist had been taking drugs – probably the poison strychnine – to help him cycle faster. Poor thing! He's famous now, not for his stunning cycling but for being the first athlete to die from taking drugs.

Jimmy Michael loved cycling too. When he worked in a butcher's shop in Aberaman he delivered meat on his bike and finished his round by riding in through the shop door to the counter without stopping. Many of the customers had a nasty shock! Jimmy broke several records:

- in 1895 for cycling 100 kilometres in 3 hours 53 minutes;
- in 1901 for cycling a mile in 1 minute 52 seconds.

Jimmy went to America to make his fortune. He died young too – at only 29 years of age, but there are no rumours that he took drugs.

THIS AND THAT

You will need a strong stomach to read this section. Make sure you have a bucket ready – just in case!

1. A Terrifying Tale

In 1876 an awful scandal broke out in Caio, Carmarthenshire. Squire John Johnes of Dolau Cothi mansion was shot dead by his butler, Henry Tremble. Tremble also shot all his master's hunting dogs and tried to murder his daughter. Then he went away and shot himself.

Squire Johnes was buried respectably in the family grave in Caio churchyard. Then, at the dead of night, Tremble's body was buried in a corner of the same churchyard. But the villagers of Caio were furious. They opened the grave, stole Tremble's body and carried it to Llanddulas graveyard to be buried. When they arrived at Llanddulas, they were met by a crowd of angry protesters, who threatened to whip anyone who tried to bury Tremble in their graveyard. The people of Llanddulas grabbed the body and carried it back to Caio. But where is Tremble's body now? Was he re-buried in Caio? The people of Caio say 'No', but they won't tell you where his body lies either.

And when they want to threaten naughty village children they say:

2. Childish Cheats

But WHO was cheating on WHOM?

Read this story about Sarah Jacob from Llanfihangel-ar-Arth and YOU decide:

Come and see

AN AMAZING SIGHT * A MIRACLE!
Sarah Jacob (12 years old)

Lletherneuadd Ucha, Llanfihangel-ar-Arth

who has lived without food or water for two whole years!

Sarah's parents, Evan and Hannah Jacob, will welcome you warmly. No charge – but the family accepts gifts.

And they came – from far and near – to stare at little Sarah Jacob fasting (and they left their gifts at the bottom of the bed).

And then dubious doctors and nosey nurses from Guy's Hospital, London, heard about the miraculous maiden in Llanfihangel-ar-Arth. Down they came at once to

Wales to see this strange phenomenon. The nurses kept their beady eyes on Sarah, day and night . . . to make sure that she didn't eat or drink anything. (No slipping down to the fridge for a quick lollipop or sausage.)

I hope I can find a man with long enough legs to wear this stocking!

To keep awake all night the nosey nurses knitted and gossiped round the bed.

Within eight days, poor little Sarah had died. (Surprise, surprise!) But whose fault was it?

★ On 15 March 1870, Evan and Hannah Jacob were sentenced to imprisonment in Carmarthen gaol – Evan to a year with hard labour and Hannah to six months. (Not very long for killing their daughter, perhaps?) Did they realise that silly Sarah had been stealing food on the sly for several years?

★ The doctors and nurses? Their job was to keep Sarah alive, not to kill her! They knew very well that no one could survive on thin air.

★ Sarah herself? When they dissected her stomach (when she was dead, of course!) there was some food in it. Had she been cheating all along and deceiving everyone before the nurses arrived to keep watch over her?

3. Top of the Pops

The Appalling Victorians of Wicked Wales loved to sing pointless popular songs. And here are the fashionable favourites. But which was NUMBER ONE in the Victorian pop charts?

SOSBAN FACH: a stupid song with daft lyrics about Mary Ann hurting her finger and Dafydd the servant being sick! And why was the baby in the cradle crying, and why had the cat scratched Joni Bach? Who cares? But Mynyddog (Mountain Man)'s song was a fashionable favourite in Llanelli, because it was about a little saucepan and a big saucepan and they made lots of saucepans in that saucy town. That's why Llanelli was called '**Tin**opolis', not because there were tin policemen there. This song was the Number One in the Top of the Pops charts in Llanelli, especially in the rugby club. The second verse, about Dai Bach the soldier with his shirt hanging out, is even worse rubbish!

GOD BLESS THE PRINCE OF WALES: A posh song in praise of Edward (or Bertie to his Mam), the Prince of Wales, the English throne and British glory. Bertie wasn't very popular with the people of Wales (Queen Vic wasn't all that keen on her son, either), because he liked gambling, drinking, playing cards and chasing women.

Dirty Bertie, I'll teach you a lesson!

LAND OF MY FATHERS: this pop song was written in 1856 by a father and son team: Evan and James James of Pontypridd. Evan's brother had emigrated to America and the lyrics tell us why Evan decided to stay at home in Wales (no gambling, drinking, women . . . no chance – read the words!). James composed the tune as he wandered with his harp along the banks of the river Rhondda (very romantic, until you recall that it was full of rubbish and sewage!). They didn't compose anything else worth writing home about.

Three starry Victorian pop songs. Which one was Top of the Pops?
✗ not Llanelli's daft ditty!
✗ not the posh pretender!

NUMBER 1: 'Land of My Fathers' was Top of the Pops in the Appalling Victorian Age. And that's why it is the Welsh National Anthem today.

I refuse to get up until you sing 'Land of my Mothers . . .'!

AMEN

So we've come to the end of our riveting tales
Of Appalling Victorians in Wicked Wales.

We'll read no more about rioters shot,
Or Rebecca's Daughters and their sad lot;

Or the lies and jibes of the rotten Blue Books,
Or hanging martyrs and transported crooks.

We've had enough of mining disasters
And the stubborn pride of the Quarry Masters.

Let's leave behind the strange superstitions,
The useless schools and the crazy customs.

★   ★   ★   ★   ★

Yet, remember too as we leave this stage,
That Queen Vic survived to a ripe old age.

Wales changed dramatically during her reign,
With new inventions – including the train,

The motor car, telephone and camera,
Gas, electricity and the cinema.

And more . . . and more . . .

And that brings us to the end of the Appalling
Victorians. I wonder what Wicked Wales will get up to
in the twentieth century?

Read all about it in *Woeful Wales at War*!